Judicial Review
in State Supreme Courts

SUNY series
in
American Constitutionalism

Robert J. Spitzer, Editor

Judicial Review in State Supreme Courts

A Comparative Study

Laura Langer

State University of New York Press

Published by
State University of New York Press, Albany

© 2002 State University of New York

For information, address the State University of New York Press,
90 State Street, Suite 700, Albany, NY 12207

Production by Michael Haggett
Marketing by Jennifer Giovani

Library of Congress Cataloging-in-Publication Data

Langer, Laura, 1965–
    Judicial review in state Supreme Courts : a comparative study / Laura Langer.
        p. cm. — (SUNY series in American constitutionalism)
    Includes bibliographical references and index.
    ISBN 0-7914-5251-4 (alk. paper) — ISBN 0-7914-5252-2 (pbk. : alk. paper)
    1. Judicial review—United States—States. I. Title. II. Series.

    KF4575.L33 2002
    347.73'12—dc21   2001049517

10 9 8 7 6 5 4 3 2 1

To my family and in memory of
John Patrick Langer.

Contents

Tables

Figures

Preface

We often think of our Congress, president, state legislature and governor as sources of the policies that affect our daily lives; yet, the final word on many policy issues is in the hands of state supreme courts. Contributing to the finality of state supreme court decisions is the minuscule number of decisions reviewed by the United States Supreme Court. Despite the important role state supreme courts play in society and the enormous value to be gained by studying judges on these courts, scholarly attention often focuses on the United States Supreme Court. It is the premise of this book that there is a substantial imbalance between the importance of state supreme courts in American politics, and the extent of our knowledge and understanding of how these institutions function and how these judges make decisions.

This book is an attempt to bridge a growing and alarming gap between American state courts and the amount of scholarly attention to these important institutions in both the literature and the classroom. Along the way, I hope to show that systematic examination of judges on state supreme courts across different areas of law can advance our conceptualization of the judiciary and offer a more general theory about judicial behavior, accountability, and the role of courts in society.

The book begins by giving an overview of judicial review by courts and explores the interplay among branches of state government in this adversarial process. In this first chapter, I lay the foundation for the proposition that judicial review is shaped by the pursuit of political ambitions, the institutional rules and arrangements governing judicial behavior in the state, and the nature of the policy adjudicated before the court.

Chapter two examines four influential conceptualizations of judicial behavior, offering divergent perspectives about the degree to which judges are, and, should be, autonomous actors. I begin with a jurisprudential perspective that contends judges are influenced by legal doctrine and case facts. A second conceptualization posits judicial behavior as a function of personal attitudes in which justices' sincere preferences guide decisions (i.e., the Attitudinal Model). Third, I discuss an institutional approach to judicial behavior, which posits that judges are influenced by rules and institutional arrangements. Finally, a strategic explanation of judicial behavior is discussed whereby judges are placed in a separation-of-powers game with other branches of government, for example. According to this judicial conceptualization, fear of retaliation from the other governmental branches serves as a check on the actions of judges.

A theory of state supreme court judicial responsiveness to the other branches of government is presented in chapter three. Here, I provide a discussion of the institutional rules, constitutional designs, and political contexts in the American states that afford other branches of state government mechanisms to punish judges for objectionable decisions. This chapter takes a closer look at electoral and policy motivations of judges and offers reasons for judicial review. I conceptualize judicial behavior in terms of ideological and institutional/contextual safety zones, which are defined by the preference distributions, institutional rules, and political settings operating in a judge's external environment.

Drawing from theoretical foundations, I lay out the hypotheses to be tested in both the agenda-setting stage and decision-on-the-merits stage of judicial review. Using some of the opinions from the state supreme court cases analyzed in the book, I provide examples of the political interactions and relationships between the judiciary and the state legislature and governor. I also provide a discussion of the constitutional designs and political contexts in the American states that afford other branches of government mechanisms to punish judges for their actions. Specifically, variations across states and over time in method of judicial retention, judicial term length, state constitutional amendment procedures, ideological distance between judges and state government, and instances of divided government between the legislature and governor are discussed in relation to political ambitions and expected strategic behavior.

In chapter four, I argue that some areas of law summon actors who pose more formidable threats to the legislature and governor and, as a result, justices may become legislative or gubernatorial targets. I offer a theory of why judicial review, and judicial voting in particular, is expected to vary across policy saliency. I begin with Robert Dahl's original contention that United States Supreme Court Justices behave differently in judicial review cases, depending on the importance of the policy to Congress. Building from Dahl's discussion, and theories about policy typologies and policies and agendas, I conceptualize areas of law in terms of the scope of conflict (i.e., players involved), and the type of conflict (i.e., ideological clarity of issue). Using this conceptualization, I propose a framework that places policies along a continuum ranging from most to least salient to the elected elite. The last section of chapter four is devoted to the selection of cases, the research design, and methodology.

Chapter five presents results for models of strategic behavior across four areas of law. The findings clearly indicate that policy and electoral threats, in many instances, severely inhibit judicial actions. Results also demonstrate that strategic behavior, and judicial review varies considerably across policy saliency. Areas of law more closely tied to the pursuit of legislative and executive political ambitions induced the most strategic behavior. Moreover, when institutional rules or political conditions increase the threat of legislative and gubernatorial retaliation, judicial behavior appears to be highly constrained.

The book concludes with an assessment of state supreme court policymaking and strategic behavior across the different areas of law. I weigh the evidence with respect to conceptualizations of judicial behavior and assess their applicability to state supreme court behavior. Three fundamental points about judicial review are made. First, an examination of the judiciary in isolation from other branches of government limits our understanding of judicial review. State supreme courts do not operate as singularly powerful policymaking institutions. The second point emphasizes the necessity to examine both agenda-setting and decision-on-the-merits stages, controlling for selection biases. The comparisons across models within each area of law demonstrate that in three of four areas of law the vote on the merits is fundamentally tied to the agenda-setting processes for state supreme courts. As a result, the conclusions drawn about state supreme courts and their policymaking ability and strategic behavior are incomplete unless both stages of the process are considered. Third, this comparative inquiry demonstrates that judicial preferences, fear of policy retaliation, and electoral vulnerability shape state supreme court justice behavior.

Acknowledgments

Of course there are many to whom I am grateful and indebted to for assistance in developing my thinking and writing this book. Much of the material in this book was initially presented as conference papers as part of my doctoral dissertation. In writing the dissertation, I have benefited tremendously from working with Paul Brace. He has been an outstanding mentor, a terrific friend, and a wonderful collaborator. I am especially grateful for the support he has given me on this and other projects. Melinda Gann Hall, Charles Barrilleaux, Henry Glick, Fran Berry, and Bill Berry also provided invaluable comments and support along the way. The wisdom and knowledge of these individuals has enhanced my scholarly development and understanding of the courts, and the relations between courts and other governmental actors.

In presenting my work, I also benefited from scholars who commented on some portions of the manuscript at professional conferences in their capacity as panel discussant or chair: Brad Canon, Jack Knight, Jennifer Segal, Chuck Shipan, Steven Smith, and Harold Spaeth. I also must thank my colleagues at the University of Arizona, without whose help this book could never have been completed. I am especially grateful for the comments, advice, and support of Brian Crisp, Bill Dixon, Brad Jones, Bill Mishler, Barb Norrander, and Lyn Ragsdale.

Finally, I am thankful for the financial support provided by the following institutions: The National Science Foundation, through grant SBR#9710082; Florida State University, through a dissertation grant and the graduate program; and Rice University, through a research fellowship.

Chapter One

The Judiciary in a System of Checks and Balances

Over one hundred and fifty years ago Alexis de Tocqueville commented that, "Scarcely any political question arises in the United States that is not resolved, sooner or later, into a judicial question."[1] Tocqueville's astute observation could not be truer today, especially with respect to courts in the American states. The expansion of rights in state constitutions and devolution of federal authority to state governments has placed American state courts in center stage of the public policymaking arena.

A growing number of legal disputes are being addressed in state supreme courts, with these courts adjudicating an inexhaustible array of novel issues. While it is common to think of our Congress, president, state legislature or governor as sources of the policies that affect our daily lives, it is clear that the final word on many issues of public policy is in the hands of each state's highest court. In 1996 for example, state supreme courts decided an average of eleven constitutional challenges to state laws and invalidated an average of two laws in each state. These judicial actors provide an alternative vehicle for making public policy in the American states and a mechanism to protect individual rights and liberties beyond the protection afforded by the United States Constitution. Increasingly judges on these state courts of last resort are called upon to determine the constitutional fate of state legislation across a range of policy. As a result, many policies governing the daily lives of citizens are resolved by the votes of state supreme court justices; these actors often become the final arbiters of state public policy.

United States Supreme Court Justice Brennan once observed, "[o]ur states are not provinces of an all powerful central government. They are political units with hard-core constitutional status and with plenary governmental responsibility for much that goes on within their borders. . . . [we] should remind ourselves that it is state court decisions which finally determine the overwhelmingly aggregate of all legal controversies in this nation" (Brennan 1996, 225). More recently, a prominent scholar of American state courts commented, "[w]ith the power to resolve the vast proportion of the nation's legal disputes, and with recent shifts in federal-state relations, the ability of state courts to affect the distribution of wealth and power in the United States is at a zenith" (Hall 1999, 115). Another judicial scholar similarly observed, "[w]ith the heavy measure of appellate judicial policy-making taking place in the states, combined with the swing toward decentralization within the American federal system, a whole new (or actually, renewed) chapter in the study of American judiciary is opening up for scholar and practitioner alike" (Stumpf 1998, 376).

The presidential election of 2000 provides a very recent example of the awesome power of state supreme courts and the expansion of their role in the policy process. This close election summoned the Florida Supreme Court into the controversy; the process asked the Florida Supreme Court to interpret Florida's election laws. In their decision, the Florida Supreme Court extended the deadline for ballot recounts that were underway in some Florida counties. This ruling was contrary to the preferences of presidential candidate Governor George W. Bush; yet in sync with presidential candidate Vice President Al Gore.

Attorneys representing George W. Bush argued the Florida Supreme Court decision violated the United States Constitution and federal law. On national television, Bush implied that the members of the Florida Supreme Court acted like legislators and complained that the state court had usurped legislative authority from the state legislative and executive branch. On the other side of the ideological spectrum, Gore and his team of attorneys, claimed victory and argued that the role of the Florida Supreme Court is to interpret the laws. If policy is made as a result of judicial statutory interpretation, Gore and his associates insisted that citizens must abide by that policy.[2]

From the above discussion, it is hard to deny the growing importance of state supreme court justices in the policy arena, particularly the role of these actors in adjudicating constitutional cases. Yet, some of the most basic information about state supreme court justices remains unknown. The expanding breadth and importance of state supreme court involvement in public policy and, in particular, judicial review contributes to the centrality of state supreme court decisions in American politics. Questions concerning state supreme court justices as policymakers, the conditions under which these judges exercise judicial review, and the interplay among state supreme court justices, legislatures, and governors are long overdue for scholarly inquiry. A pertinent question, for example, is why some state supreme court justices give greater deference to the legislated will, while others seem to expand their authority by seeking opportunities to invalidate state laws.

The goal of this book is to begin to fill a gap in our knowledge about the policymaking role of state supreme court justices and shed light on whether or not justices on these courts have unchecked powers in the agenda-setting stage and the decision-on-the-merits stage of judicial review. Along the way, I hope to advance a more general theory about judicial interactions with other governmental actors. From a broader perspective, the relationship among the three branches of state government is assessed through a systematic, comparative examination of how separation-of-powers and state constitutional designs might constrain or facilitate judicial review.

Examination of the exercise of judicial review by state supreme court justices can tell us whether these judges are responsive to the legislature and governor directly. Assessing the degree of judicial independence from other branches of government also indicates whether or not judges are accountable to the public, albeit indirectly. The extent to which other branches of government affect judicial decisions, and differentially across areas of law, is at the core of debates about judicial independence and judicial accountability. Responsiveness thus raises serious questions about whether the judiciary should be insulated from political pressures. Thus, this study informs debates about judicial accountability, motivations of judicial behavior, and the nature of state supreme court justices as makers of public policy.

More specifically, this book addresses the following questions: (1) how other branches of government influence judicial review; (2) why the judiciary is expected to pay attention to legislative and gubernatorial preferences; (3) under what conditions state legislatures and governors influence state supreme court justices when they decide constitutional challenges to state legislation; and (4) whether or not legislative-judicial relations vary across areas of law, permitting legislatures and governors to impose greater constraints on judges in some areas of law more than others? Over four hundred docketed challenges to campaign and election laws, workers' compensation laws, unemployment compensation laws, and welfare laws during the 1970–1993 time period are examined. Additionally, explanations accounting for variation in twenty-three hundred votes to invalidate or uphold statutes in four policy areas are provided. Attention is focused on four different areas of law known to summon distinct actors to the policy arena and cultivate different political relationships in this process.

The primary argument forwarded in this book is that the presence of challenges to state legislation on state supreme court dockets and judges' votes to invalidate legislation varies across areas of law because the stakes in the game differ, depending on the policy. Stated differently, the extent to which state legislatures and governors influence judicial review depends upon the saliency of the policy area. The relationship between the area of law and the pursuit of political ambitions by the legislature and governor is found to be critical. A fundamental point is that state supreme court justices are most likely to serve as legitimizing agents of the legislature and governor when the issue is of critical import to the legislature and governor or when institutional rules and political environment tie judges' fortunes to other branches of government.

A natural starting point for an examination of state supreme court policymaking begins with the origin of judicial review and the debates surrounding this important policymaking function. In the section that follows, some of the main points of contention about the proper role of the judiciary and its use of judicial review are discussed, with an emphasis on the United States Supreme Court. This summary provides a framework from which we can examine this behavior in state supreme courts.

COURTS AS POLICYMAKERS

The United States Supreme Court assumed a monitoring role over governmental actions in 1803 when the Court found section 13 of the Judiciary Act of 1789 in violation of the U.S. Constitution (*Marbury v. Madison*) ICR. 137 (1803). The doctrine of judicial review, formulated in the *Marbury* decision, gave the judiciary, in this case the United States Supreme Court, the power to invalidate laws that conflict with the principles of the Constitution. Technically, judicial review authorizes courts to constitutionally review the actions of other branches, and assess whether or not such actions, legislation for example, violate state constitutions or the federal Constitution. This notion of judicial supremacy affords each judge, especially those serving on high courts, awesome policymaking powers.

Quite simply, judicial review is viewed as a tool for judges to check governmental actions on constitutional grounds. Judicial review also affords judges the opportunity to unmake public policy. In *Mitchell v. Steffen* 504 N.W. 2d 198 (1993), the Supreme Court of Minnesota declared unconstitutional a Minnesota statute that imposed durational residency requirements on recipients of general assistance work readiness benefits. Here the state supreme court superceded the legislative will to restrict and reduce welfare spending in Minnesota.

Judicial review also gives judges the opportunity to reinforce the status quo (or current policy) and influence the direction of future policy. For example, in *Jones v. Milwaukee County* 485 N.W. 2d 21 (1992) the Wisconsin Supreme Court held that sixty-day waiting period requirements for welfare assistance were constitutional under the equal protection clause of the United

States and Wisconsin Constitutions. This judicial review case not only validated (or legitimized) residency requirements in other Wisconsin counties, but the court's decision also led the way for additional residency restrictions on welfare in other states.

These examples demonstrate that fundamentally, state judicial review decisions affect the lives of the citizenry, influence the nature of existing public policy, and shape the course of future public policy. Additionally, the outcomes in judicial review cases can hinder or advance the budgetary capacity of state governments. Lastly, judicial review decisions can impede or facilitate the political ambitions of governmental actors.

Critical to a discussion about judicial review is the premise that judicial review permits nonelected branches of government to frustrate or replace the majority will. However, scholars also have argued that the system of checks and balances contributes to the Court's ability to play a unique role as protector of minority and individual rights through its power of judicial review (see, e.g., Dye and Zeigler 1972). In this way, the authority and unimpeded ability of courts to monitor governmental actions can protect individuals against a tyranny of majority and impede constitutional violations of rights and freedoms. Quite simply, judicial review affords judges a tool that allows them to protect individuals from arbitrary governmental action. According to one legal scholar, such judicial supremacy ensures "that, at the end of the day, judges free of congressional and executive control will be in a position to determine whether the assertion of power against the citizen is consistent with law (including the Constitution)" (Bator 1990, 267).

The foci of this book are the conditions under which judges engage in judicial review and the conditions under which judges are most and least likely to invalidate laws. When do judges, for example, act as if they are free from legislative and executive control? These simple questions lie at the heart of fundamental debates that have ensued about the role of the judiciary in a democracy, and in particular, the degree to which courts have invalidated statutes. For example, Robert Dahl (1957) argued that United States Supreme Court Justices rarely challenge federal laws because "the frequency and nature of appointments to the United States Supreme Court prohibits it from playing this role" (1989, 598). Besides the appointment process, Dahl argued that the importance of an issue to the current lawmaking majority affected the willingness of Congress to react to the United States Supreme Court via statutory or constitutional amendment. As a result, the importance of the issue shapes the interplay between the United States Supreme Court and Congress.

Richard Funston (1975) also argued that the United States Supreme Court rarely invalidated statutes, because the recruitment process placed judges on the bench whose preferences were consonant with the president and the median members of Congress. Consistent with Robert Dahl and Richard Funston, John Gates (1987) demonstrated that the United States Supreme Court is more likely to overturn state statutes when the majority on the Court differed from the party in control of state government at the time the law was enacted.

Overall, these scholars have argued that the United States Supreme Court behaves in a countermajoritarian fashion only when the preferences of the Supreme Court and the other branches of government conflict. They believed that the recruitment process guaranteed that the Supreme Court would legitimate the preferences of the current lawmaking majority.[3]

While debates over the exercise of judicial review continue, scholars have noted that the nation's highest court seems to have shifted some important decision making to American state courts (see e.g, Hall 1999; Brace, Hall, Langer 2001). Other scholars have long-documented the important and rising role of state supreme courts as makers of public policy via the power of judicial review (Sheldon 1987; Emmert 1992).

STATE SUPREME COURT JUDICIAL REVIEW

In the past few years alone, the United States Supreme Court has greatly circumscribed Congress' ability to make federal laws binding on the American states, directly shaping the nature of state politics. For example, in a series of decisions since 1996, the Supreme Court has expanded states' rights and limited federal power over the states in several important policy areas, such as the regulation of business, the right to sue, the regulation of campaign contributions and election systems, and civil rights issues.[4] Recently, one legal scholar observed that the decisions by the United States Supreme Court in 1999, "have extended the immunity of states beyond a mere limit on federal judicial power into a natural and indigenous right of sovereignty with an uncertain scope" (James 1999, 10).

This shift of decision making to the American states focuses attention on judicial review by state supreme courts. In many ways judicial review by state supreme courts is a continuation of the debate about democratic theory and accountability that has ensued at the United States Supreme Court level. The ability of judges to frustrate the legislated will of majorities and challenge statutes on constitutional grounds, however, takes on new dimensions when examined in state supreme courts. Consequently, scholars can systematically test hypotheses about the policymaking role of judges and the relationship between judges and other branches of government across a host of institutional settings and degrees of accountability. Such inquires cannot be done at the national level simply because variation in important rules, constitutional designs, and settings is either rare or nonexistent. One of the advantages of my test of the separation-of-powers model to assess the interplay among the judiciary, legislature, and executive branch, is that in the American states there are stronger reasons for policy retaliation from state government, especially in judicial review cases, and there are reasons for judges to worry about electoral retaliation from state government. Hence while the separation-of-powers models: (1) cannot be applied to interactions between Congress and the United States Supreme Court in *judicial review cases* (i.e., overriding a constitutional amendment requires consideration of state legislatures as well); (2) cannot assume *policy as well as electoral motivations* of judges when tested on interactions between Congress and the United States Supreme Court; and (3) has not been tested across varying institutional rules, in the American states these limitations do not exist.

The exercise of judicial review, viewed by some as a threat to democratic government, might be encouraged by the constitutional designs in some states. For example, like members of the United States Supreme Court, some state supreme court justices are more insulated from the political pressures of other governmental branches. Conversely, constitutional designs, institutional rules, and the nature of political systems in the American states can mitigate the dangers of countermajoritarian behavior. The practice of constitutional amendment passage by state legislatures for example is fundamentally different from Congress. Unlike constitutional decisions made by the United States Supreme Court, state supreme court constitutional decisions are relatively easy to override via constitutional amendment. The average amendment rate in the American states is 1.23 amendments per year compared to only .13 per year for the U.S. Constitution (Lutz 1994, 367). Indeed eight states averaged two or more constitutional amendments per year. Moreover, state legislatures utilize the amendment procedure routinely; ninety-one percent of amendments in the American states during 1970 to 1979 were initiated by the legislature (Lutz 1994, 360; see also Hammons 1999). Depending on institutional rules, context, and political settings, state supreme court justices might act as faithful agents of the state legislature and governor. Judges on these courts might be less likely to challenge the will of legislative majorities, when confronted with politically threatening situations that increase fears of policy or electoral retaliation from the legislature and governor. In these instances, one might say a "majoritarian difficulty" becomes a potential concern for democratic theory because these judges, fearful of retaliation from other branches of government, might ignore constitutional grievances or legal harms committed against minorities in an effort to keep in sync with the ruling elite.

From this complex political milieu in the American states, appropriate questions for judicial scholars include, to whom are judges beholden, to what extent, and under what conditions? Systematic examination of the extent to which state supreme court justices make public policy through the exercise of judicial review, and under what conditions, is thus critical and timely. This book offers the first assessment of these questions pertaining to whether or not state supreme court justices are beholden to state legislatures and governors across four areas of law. Of course, if judicial review in state supreme courts does not vary across states, over time, and across areas of law, the benefits of a systematic, comparative study of this nature are few. A brief look at the use of judicial review by state supreme courts is offered in the next section to emphasize the variation that exists.

EVOLUTION OF JUDICIAL REVIEW
IN STATE SUPREME COURTS

One of the most important ways state supreme courts make public policy is through their power of judicial review. While other ways exist for state supreme courts to make public policy (see, e.g., Canon 1983), reviewing and invalidating state laws is perhaps the most intrusive and salient mechanism by which judges can translate their preferences into public policy. Many view invalidating laws as heightened judicial activism.

Charles Sheldon noted that, "even before Chief Justice Marshall's reaffirmation of this power for the nation's high court in *Marbury v. Madison* (1803), a number of state courts had negated acts of their legislature" (1987, 71). In his examination of the evolution of judicial review from 1890 to 1986 in state supreme courts and, in particular, Washington's state supreme court, Sheldon also found that state high courts began exercising an increasingly active role in the policymaking process starting in the late 1970s.

Sheldon also noted that a different function of judicial review had emerged over time. In his study, for example, he observed that judicial review by state supreme courts had typically been used as a defensive mechanism to protect courts from legislative or gubernatorial encroachments of power.[5] This protection mechanism was considered to be a fundamental tenet in the American judicial system, providing a safety device to dissuade elected persons from temptations to abuse power. For example, when state legislatures engaged in activities that were constitutionally delegated to the executive branch, judicial review allowed judges to stop abuses of this kind.

Similarly judicial review allowed judges to prevent the executive or legislative branches from taking power away from the courts. Here the courts invalidated laws that determined appellate procedures or dictated sentencing guidelines, which were viewed as typical judicial responsibilities. Moreover, judicial review could be used to secure basic rights, protect citizens from governmental abuses of power, and ensure each branch of government some authority in the process (*Federalist* No. 51 and No. 78). Over time, however, Sheldon found that judicial review increasingly had become a mechanism for judges to enhance and expand their authority rather than simply protect the judicial institution and the citizenry from abuses by the other governmental branches (1987, 69).

State judicial review has oscillated between periods of judicial restraint and judicial activism. The 1970s marked a period of new judicial activism and state supreme court justices adopted a role that was exceedingly active in the 1990s (see e.g., Baum 1997). During these periods, judicial review by state supreme courts also had become both a defensive and offensive mechanism. The application of judicial review beyond protection from encroachments of power is further evidence that state supreme court justices over time have assumed a more authoritative role in making policy. Through this power, courts have maintained a veto in a system of checks and balances and broadened their authority in the policymaking process. Other judicial scholars also have noted increasing trends of judicial activism by state high courts (see, e.g., Sheldon 1987; Tarr and Porter 1988; Glick 1991). Some have referred to the expanding role of state supreme courts as new judicial federalism, noting that a growing reliance on state constitutions and an expansion of these documents has contributed to a resurgence of state supreme court power (Tarr 1998).

The degree to which courts invoke their policymaking powers and the frequency with which state supreme court justices vote to invalidate state laws varies across states, over time, and across issue areas. For example, Sheldon (1987) found that an average of one in twenty-five cases resolved by the Washington Supreme Court in the late 1970s and 1980s involved a constitutional challenge to legislation. Of these cases, the Washington Supreme Court invalidated one out of every four statutes (Sheldon 1987, 89), with the number of unanimous decisions varying over this time period. Susan Fino (1987) found that state courts of last resort during the 1975 and 1984 period were more likely to invalidate statutes; on average, state supreme courts upheld only 22.7 percent of equal protection challenges (Fino 1987, 62). This marked a significant rise in the number of laws invalidated on equal protection grounds by state supreme court judges.

In a more comprehensive study, Craig F. Emmert found that state supreme courts decided over three thousand judicial review cases between 1981 and 1985 (Emmert 1992, 549). Of these cases, the state statutes that were challenged before the courts were declared unconstitutional almost 20 percent of the time (Emmert 1992, 551) and the likelihood of a court overturning a state law varied, depending on the policy issue.

Emmert also observed tremendous variation across states in the propensity of these courts to review and invalidate state statutes. For example, Emmert found that the Georgia Supreme Court decided the constitutionality of statutes in 165 judicial review cases during the 1981 through 1985 period, while Hawaii's high court heard only twenty-one judicial review cases during this same period (cited in Glick 1991, 100). More recently, Russell S. Harrison and G. Alan Tarr (1996) noted that twenty-two state supreme courts reviewed constitutional challenges to school finance systems during the 1973 through 1993 period. Of these states, twelve courts rejected the constitutional challenge and ten courts found the systems violated constitutional mandates. Since 1989 alone, four state supreme courts invalidated school-finance programs (Harrison and Tarr 1996, 179).

Turning to the cases examined in this book, during the 1970–1993 time period, state supreme court justices decided the constitutional fate of over four-hundred pieces of state legislation in just four areas of law (i.e., campaign and election law, workers' compensation law, unemployment compensation law, and welfare law). In some instances, the outcome of the court decision was to uphold the state law; yet, in other states, the court invalidated similar legislation. The individual votes of judges in these cases also reveal interesting patterns. For example, some state supreme court justices voted to uphold the legislation being challenged, while other judges on the same court voted to overturn the legislation. Moreover, some state supreme court justices wished to avoid certain policy issues, while tackling issues willingly in other areas of law.

Clearly there are differences in the occurrence of these cases on state supreme court dockets, the propensity of courts to overturn legislation, and the likelihood of judges voting to invalidate laws. These variations in judicial votes raise a host of important, yet unanswered, questions about judicial review in state supreme courts. This book sheds light on why challenges to state legislation occur on some state supreme court dockets, but not others. This book also addresses why some judges assert an active role in the policymaking arena, striking down state laws, and other judges exercise much more restraint.

By looking at the timing of docketed judicial review cases and patterns of votes by individual judges deciding state constitutional cases across four areas of law, this book identifies how the interplay among judicial, legislative, and gubernatorial ambition affect voting behavior and subsequently public policy. From this examination, a broader understanding of the motivations of judicial behavior and policymaking under various constitutional designs and institutional settings is possible. Moreover, a better understanding of how judges react to the legislature and governor as well as whether judges seek to legitimize the actions of other governmental branches can be gained. The next section lays the foundation for the proposition that legislative and gubernatorial interests can and do shape judicial review.

ADVERSARIAL NATURE OF JUDICIAL REVIEW:
ITS IMPLICATIONS ON VOTING

While the scope of some or even many court reversals may be quite narrow, invalidations of state law are nonetheless instances when state supreme courts supersede legislatures with their own policy preferences. In these cases, state supreme court justices usurp policymaking authority from other branches of government, and become the final arbiter of policy, at least in the short run. Essentially, they are exercising their prerogative in the system of checks and balances created by the separation of powers common in American government and state constitutions.

Clearly this is an adversarial process likely to evoke conflict and retaliation from the other actors involved in the policymaking game. Chief Justice, Shirley S. Abrahamson, of the Wisconsin Supreme Court observed "[l]egislators do not universally welcome judges in the legislative process. Some legislators express resentment toward judges' incursions into their domain . . ." (1996, 82). Consider also the remark by state Supreme Court Chief Justice, Judith S. Kaye on the New York Court of Appeals, "No one can question the legislature's authority to correct or redirect a state court's interpretation of a statute. Indeed, on our court we especially strive for consensus in statutory interpretation cases as a matter of policy, knowing that the legislature always can, and will, step in if it feels we have gotten it wrong" (Kaye, 1995, 23). Judges are even more concerned about legislative retaliation in constitutional cases.

Observations made by other state supreme court justices and legislators also demonstrate the contentious, tit-for-tat nature of judicial review. Superior Court Chief Justice Joseph Nadeau of New Hampshire was quoted as saying, " . . . [w]hen removal is threatened for the kind of conduct that is *expected* of a judge, judicial independence is compromised. When there is legislative retaliation for decisions, independence is compromised" (Wise, 1999, 22). Recognizing the reality of a system of checks and balances, Chief Justice Ellen Ash Peters' of Connecticut's high court stated, "courts are not ivory towers, sheltered from the vicissitudes of everyday life and controversy . . . [state court judges work] in an adversarial context, facing a relentless tide of new cases" (cited in Kaye 1995, 4). Moreover, Daniel Blue, speaker of the North Carolina House once noted that, "[t]he political environment in which we operate can be divisive, both within and between the branches of government. . . . Many judges are elected or at least retained at the polls and therefore are not removed from the political processes faced by those of us in representative government" (Blue 1991, 34).

Combined these comments indicate that the relationships among state governmental actors is one characterized by political pressure, political games, and contentious behavior. These comments also imply that state supreme court justices, legislators, and governors pursue political ambitions (e.g., electoral or policy goals) that might be hindered by other governmental actors.

The system of checks and balances ties political ambitions pursued by judges to the ambitions of the other government actors. While each branch of government works against the other, they also must work together. Paul Brace and Barbara Hinkley (1992) in their book on the presidency remind us of the unfriendly relationship between Congress and the president. They observe, " . . . a political cartoonist showed an elegant president poised on a tennis court, racket in hand. Across the net was a heavyset, unshaven opponent, Congress, clutching a bowling ball" (Brace and Hinkley 1992, 72). Given the anecdotes shared by state supreme court justices, legislators, and scholars, it seems that a similar cartoon including the judiciary is appropriate. In states where the judiciary is insulated from political pressures, such a cartoon would depict the legislatures and governors holding the racket on the tennis court with state supreme courts clutching a bowling ball. However, in states where the judiciary is directly tied to the other branches of government, the cartoon would depict state supreme courts holding the racket and the legislative and executive branches with the bowling ball.

Judges, legislators, and governors have incentives to pay attention to each other's actions. They also have reasons to engage in tactics that keep the other in line, or at least out of harms way. The interplay between judges and the other branches of government can be detrimental to the careers of the actors involved in the game of judicial review. The stakes also are much higher in these constitutional cases where legislators watch more closely the actions of judges as these judges decide the ultimate fate of legislation.

PAST APPROACHES TO STUDYING
STATE SUPREME COURTS AS POLICYMAKERS

Despite the importance of judicial review as a policymaking tool and the political nature and significance of this activity, the causes and consequences of judicial review have received scant attention in the American states. Moreover, extant literature on state supreme courts as policymakers, while informative, has been primarily historical and descriptive. Most research employs cross-sectional approaches that study one or several issues at a single point in time or longitudinal designs of single states or a single issue (see e.g., Sheldon 1987, Tarr and Porter 1988, Glick 1991). Alan G. Tarr and Mary Cornelia Aldis Porter's (1988) study provides one of the best comparative accounts of state supreme courts in their policymaking roles, adopting primarily a case-study approach that emphasizes the important intricacies of the fifty-two state courts of last resort (Texas and Oklahoma each have two courts of last resort, separating civil from criminal cases). Other scholars, Sheldon for example, have employed a longitudinal approach, historically documenting differences in one state over time.

Some scholars also have substantially advanced our understanding of judicial review by state supreme courts through systematical examination across states and time (see e.g., Emmert 1992); however, a common theme of previous studies is that courts are isolated from other branches of government. Stated differently, explicit tests of how and under what conditions legislatures and governors influence judicial review have not been conducted. Another shared characteristic of past approaches to state supreme court judicial review, and policymaking more generally, is a concentration on aggregate court behavior instead of individual voting patterns. Typically, these studies examine the number of cases on court dockets or the number of statutes invalidated by the court.

If we want to develop an overarching theory of judicial behavior and understand the policy role of judges, we ought to move beyond single institutions, single issues, and high levels of aggregation. Systematic examination of individual voting behavior, across policy issues, and within the context of systems of checks and balances is an important consideration that deserves attention in the judicial literature.

By ignoring how, why, and under what conditions, legislatures and governors shape the individual votes of justices in judicial review cases, we are missing important information about the policymaking process in the American states that affords each political actor some say in the process. Differences in policies across states, for example, could be due to variation in the degree to which judges are an integral part of the process. Moreover, these differences might be related to the extent to which judges are insulated from legislative and gubernatorial threats and pressures that target individual judges. The role state supreme court justices play as policymakers is thus contingent upon the interplay between courts and other branches of government.

Equally important is how differences across areas of law shape judicial review. For example, when judicial behavior varies across policy areas it suggests that certain issues are more likely to be decided by the legislature and governor, while other issues tend ultimately to be decided by the courts. Not only does this speak to the distribution of power in the policymaking arena, but also it indicates which conflicts might be advantaged or disadvantaged by court intervention. Some areas of law, for example, might encourage justices to invoke their gatekeeping powers more than other areas. In these instances, litigants who turn to the courts for resolution of their constitutional grievances might be shut out from the policymaking process.

Given that policies summon different actors to the political arena and encourage distinct interactions in and out of the policymaking process, access to courts as alternative vehicles for public policy can vary across areas of law. These differences have important ramifications for policymaking when we consider that judges might be more constrained when deciding the constitutionality of issues "near-and-dear" to elected elite. This might be especially true in states where judicial ambitions can be impeded by other branches of government. Thus, evaluation of how judicial review varies across policy saliency can help us better understand why some judges are more likely to address trivial issues while other judges are willing to address more controversial issues.

STRATEGIC VERSUS SINCERE BEHAVIOR

One of the pivotal debates in the literature on U.S. courts is the extent to which judges can and do act strategically vis-à-vis other actors. For example, scholars have posited that judicial ideology explains voting behavior in cases that pose constitutional challenges to legislation. Stated more simply, a liberal judge will vote in a liberal direction and a conservative judge will vote in a conservative direction (Segal and Spaeth 1993). This is referred to as the "Sincere Voting Hypothesis." Alternatively, scholars have argued that a judge votes a particular way because external actors (e.g., legislative branch) influenced her decision. This implies that a liberal judge is encouraged to vote in a conservative direction when an external actor is conservative, for example, because the external actor can penalize the judge for objectionable decisions (e.g., Murphy 1964; Gely and Spiller 1990; Epstein and Knight 1998). This is called the "Strategic Voting Hypothesis."

Examination of individual voting patterns across areas of law thus advances our understanding of why some policies encourage justices to alter their behavior, while other issues permit justices to vote in accordance with their own ideology. In this way, the book informs the ongoing discussion about strategic or sincere voting by members of the judiciary. In short, the benefits from an empirical, comparative examination over time and across areas of law, using both aggregate and individual level analyses, are obvious and numerous.

The American states provide an excellent opportunity to assess whether justices make strategic calculations when engaging in judicial review across four areas of law. First, states provide analytical leverage to test hypotheses about strategic behavior across a host of alternative institutional rules, designs, and competing political actors (see e.g., Brace and Hall 1995). States also provide the variation necessary to examine the forces which influence why these cases appear on some state supreme court dockets but not others. Moreover, states have many legislative and executive mechanisms for dealing with judicial decisions that declare a statute unconstitutional (Abrahamson and Hughes 1991). The myriad tools available to legislatures and governors intensify interbranch conflict and presumably increase incentives for strategic behavior and tit-for-tat games between state supreme court justices and other governmental actors.

To address questions about judicial review and strategic behavior, I begin with the premise that state supreme court justices are rational actors pursuing political ambitions, such as policy and electoral goals (see e.g., Baum, 1997, Brace, Hall, Langer 1999). I assess whether these pursuits affect state supreme court justices' votes on the constitutional fate of state law. I extend a separation-of-powers conceptualization of the judiciary to consider dual goals that state supreme court justices pursue.

An important feature of state political systems is that state supreme court justices operate under a variety of electoral and institutional constraints. In the American states some justices are fearful they will be held accountable to the legislature and governor for their votes, because these branches have the power to supersede the preferences of an individual judge, for example, over-riding that judge's vote with a constitutional amendment. Additionally, in some states, the legislature and governor have the authority to retain judges. In these states, a judge's electoral fate is directly in the hands of the legislature and governor.

This book thus considers both policy and electoral fears that might shape the relationship among state supreme courts, the legislature, and the governor. Which, as a result, influence strategic behavior. I argue that when institutional rules, such as method of retention, and political conditions, such as ease in amendment passage, facilitate retaliation, justices are expected to engage in strategic behavior. These rules and contexts can make it easier for other branches of government to remove justices from the bench or reverse a judge's vote through constitutional amendment. The central issue underlying this conceptualization of judicial review is whether or not justices are induced to vote strategically vis-à-vis other political institutions.

A COMPARATIVE APPROACH TO JUDICIAL AUTONOMY AND STATE JUDICIAL REVIEW

Scholarly inquiry on state supreme court judicial review fails to advance a theory that accounts for variation of judicial review across areas of law within the context of a policymaking game. Moreover, with few exceptions, scholars have not empirically evaluated how two stages of judicial review (i.e., agenda-setting stages and decision-on-the-merits) are related. By utilizing state supreme courts as the laboratories to examine alternative explanations of judicial review, this book tests important hypotheses that have not undergone systematic evaluation.

Fundamentally, judges do not operate in a vacuum. Rather state supreme court justices are expected to alter their votes in response to the anticipated reactions from the legislature and governor. Thus, it is critical to assess how state supreme court judges interact with other governmental actors, and why judicial review might vary across areas of law, particularly due to state legislative and gubernatorial interests.

The approach utilized thus complements both attitudinal and separation of powers explanations of judicial behavior. I conceptualize state supreme court justices as if they are inside or outside of ideological and institutional/ contextual safety zones. Safety zones are defined by the degree to which preference distributions, institutional rules, and political settings tie the fate of judges' policy or electoral ambitions to other branches of government. Stated differently, the safety zone depicts the extent to which judges anticipate retribution for their voting behavior from the state legislature and governor. Strategic behavior manifests when judges alter their behavior in response to legislative and gubernatorial electoral or policy threats. For example, judges insulated from other branches of government were found to vote in accordance with their sincere policy preferences, while justices whose careers and policy ambitions were tied to the legislature and governor were found to engage in strategic behavior.

Next, I test whether or not we can generalize these types of behavior on the gamut of issues on which state supreme court justices might exercise their power of judicial review. The following four policy areas chosen are reasoned to be of varying degrees of saliency to elected elite: (1) election and campaign legislation, (2) workers' compensation legislation, (3) unemployment compensation legislation, and (4) welfare legislation. Particular attention is given to legislative and gubernatorial influence over judges to assess how constitutional designs and systems of checks and balances affect the nature of policymaking by state supreme court justices and the interplay among the three branches of government.

The crux of the argument is that state supreme court justices can be held accountable to the legislature and governor for their votes. The degree of accountability varies across policy issues. Strategic behavior thus is contingent not only upon institutional rules and designs, but also on legislative and gubernatorial ambitions, which are conditional on the area of law. As this book will show, this has important implications for policymaking in the American states; the role state supreme court justices play in this process, and the notion of strategic behavior.

This institutional approach to study judicial behavior permits an evaluation of the degree to which judges are responsive to other branches of American state government, and under what conditions. According to Douglass C. North (1990), institutions should be modeled as constraints on action, evaluating how they affect the interaction among actors and the choices available to actors. Similarly, Barry Weingast contends that studies considering the strategic interplay among the three branches of government, "show how decisions made by actors in one branch systematically depend on the sequence of interaction; and the preferences, actions, and potential actions of actors in the other branches. The potential result is a genuine theory of interaction of the major institutions of American national politics, a mature theory of the separation of powers." (Weingast 1996, 174).

Thus, it is important to utilize an approach that encompasses some of the important features of a separation-of-powers argument, accounts for the diversity across the American states, and builds upon the premise that state supreme court justices, legislators, and governors pursue similar ambitions.

ORGANIZATION OF THE STUDY

I have argued that judicial votes to review and invalidate state laws are influenced, in part, by the anticipated reaction from the legislature and governor. I have laid the foundation for the proposition that judicial review is shaped by the pursuit of political ambitions, the institutional rules and arrangements governing judicial behavior in the state, and the nature of the policy adjudicated before the court. In the next chapter, four influential conceptualizations of judicial behavior are discussed, offering divergent perspectives about judicial motivations and judicial review.

Chapter three takes a closer look at electoral and policy motivations of judges and offers several hypotheses to be tested. A theory of state supreme court responsiveness to the other branches of government is developed further.

In chapter four, how I conceptualize policy saliency is discussed. Results for models of judicial review across four areas of law are presented in chapter five and the implications of strategic and sincere behavior on judicial review are discussed in the concluding chapter.

A more complete understanding of state supreme courts in the policymaking arena is gained when we consider attitudinal and separation-of-powers explanations of judicial review, across alternative institutional rules, political settings, and competing political actors in the American states.

Chapter Two

Explanations of Judicial Behavior

Why judges behave the way they do is a perennial question of critical import to American politics and judicial behavior. Scholars have spent considerable time and effort developing theories and testing hypotheses to address this fundamental question at both stages of the judicial process: (1) agenda-setting stages and (2) decision-on-the-merits. Emerging from this literature are at least four conceptualizations of judicial behavior that are informative. These conceptualizations are developed for the purposes of this book; some scholars might place certain publications in a different venue. Moreover, it is not an exhaustive account of the literature to date.

A jurisprudential perspective posits that legal doctrine, precedent, case facts, and the like, should influence the voting behavior of judges. Research on the United States Supreme Court also has consisted of attitudinal approaches to studying judicial behavior; justices' sincere preferences guide decisions. A neo-institutional approach views judges as rational actors whose behavior is influenced by institutional rules and designs, and other conditions (or situations) that link judges to their external political environment. Finally, other studies place the United States Supreme Court in a separation-of-powers game with other branches of government, positing, for example, that fear of policy retaliation serves as a check on the actions of this Court.

A fundamental difference among these four explanations is what motivates judicial behavior. The approach in this book complements these four conceptualizations, but the primary method emphasizes a broader separation-of-powers and neo-institutional explanation.

TWO STAGES OF JUDICIAL POLICYMAKING

Scholars have examined the usefulness of these various explanations of judicial behavior across two stages of decision making. A discussion of these two stages is instructive. As illustrated in figure 2.1, the first stage of judicial review depicts the agenda-setting process or gatekeeping powers of the judiciary. In this stage, state supreme courts, for example, make decisions as to whether or not they will resolve the substantive controversy raised in the case. When a case is before the state supreme court, this indicates that litigants appealed the lower court decision to the state's court of last resort.[1] When the state supreme court renders a formal opinion, this indicates that they heard the case. Thus, a necessary condition for a case to be on the docket is that a litigant took the dispute to the state supreme court.[2]

A second important part of the agenda-setting process involves a court decision to resolve the contentions posed by the litigants. The case might get onto the court's docket, but the court can still decide whether or not it will address the substantive merits of the controversy. For example, the court might decide that the litigant has not met the requirements for the court to have a full hearing on one or any of the merits of the controversy. These thresholds (e.g., standing, mootness, jurisdiction) serve as gatekeeping mechanisms through which courts exercise control over the docket.

In addition to these common thresholds, many times state supreme courts will resolve other issues raised, avoiding or dismissing the judicial review challenge. For example, often these courts dismiss constitutional challenges to state legislation because the issue of constitutionality was not raised in the lower court. According to Gregory J. Rathjen and Harold J. Spaeth (1979, 1990), the threshold decision serves as a "second gate that litigants must pass through in order to secure resolution of their substantive contentions" (1990, 25).

In this book, agenda-setting refers to instances when courts have docketed cases in which the constitutional challenge to state law was resolved (see outcome 1a in fig. 1). Given that there were ample opportunities for every state supreme court to address constitutional challenges in all four areas of law, willingness is the issue, not opportunity. This definition of agenda-setting only differs slightly from existing studies on the United States Supreme Court. In these studies, scholarly attention focuses on the granting or denial of *certiorari*. Writs of *certiorari* are not common in American state supreme courts. Thus, simply assessing conditions under which state supreme courts grant or deny hearing a case is not possible in all fifty states. Moreover, judges on any court are not required to record their vote on the initial granting of *certiorari* or on the decision to give full hearing on merits of substantive controversy. Consequently, it is very difficult to disentangle these two votes in the agenda-setting process.

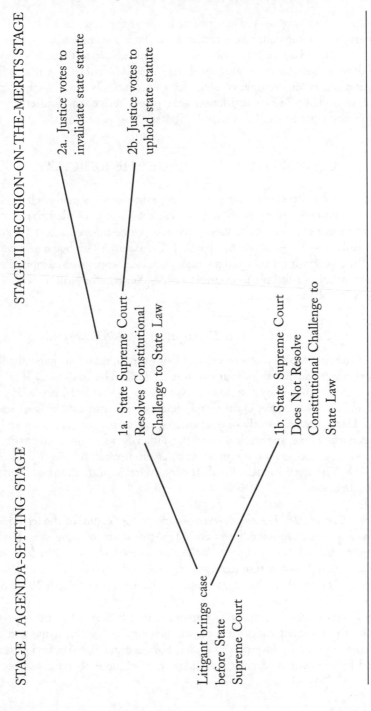

STAGE I AGENDA-SETTING STAGE   STAGE II DECISION-ON-THE-MERITS STAGE

Litigant brings case
before State
Supreme Court

1a. State Supreme Court
Resolves Constitutional
Challenge to State Law

1b. State Supreme Court
Does Not Resolve
Constitutional Challenge to
State Law

2a. Justice votes to
invalidate state statute

2b. Justice votes to
uphold state statute

Fig. 2.1. Two Stages of Judicial Review in State Supreme Courts

The second stage of judicial review involves the votes of each justice on the merits of the substantive controversy (i.e., constitutional challenge to state law).[3] A judge who casts a vote to invalidate a law restricting campaign expenditures, because it violates the First Amendment of the United States Constitution, is an example of stage two (outcome 2a, fig. 1). Similarly, a justice who strikes down legislation that places residency requirements on welfare recipients is another example of stage two.

CONCEPTUALIZATIONS OF THE JUDICIARY

Courts provide alternative venues to shape policy in the agenda-setting stage and the decision-on-the-merits stage of judicial review. While it has become relatively common practice to view judges as policy-minded actors (Pritchett 1948; Rohde and Spaeth 1976; Spaeth 1979; Baum 1985; Segal and Spaeth 1993), the proposition that judges make policy is controversial nonetheless. As such, scholars continue to examine various motives for judicial behavior in both stages of the process.

Legal and Case Fact Explanations of Judicial Behavior

One of the first explanations to emerge from the literature on judicial behavior is the legal model of judicial decision making. The traditional legal perspective posits that judges decide cases with respect to laws, precedent, and constitutions, for example. Quite simply, judges are constrained by law (Stumpf 1988). Here scholars mostly have examined the impact of case facts and law on behavior. These approaches treat the judiciary as an isolated institution and posit that judges, for the most part, are motivated by the will to make good law. The legal model also dismisses strategic and sincere accounts of judicial behavior.

Evidence from the decision-on-the-merits stage. One feature of the legal model that has received considerable attention is the norm of *stare decisis*, which most generally requires judges to adhere to precedent. A preponderance of evidence, though not without controversy, suggests judges vote according to preferences rather than this legal principle (Brenner and Spaeth 1995; Segal and Spaeth 1993, Spaeth and Segal 1999).

Scholars working within this jurisprudential framework contend that in addition to precedent, judges are constrained by the legal doctrine and constitutional arguments governing the case. For example, the standard of review applied by the court is expected to shape the outcome of the case. Another feature of a legal model of judicial behavior focuses on how the facts of the case influence votes. Scholars have found some support for the influence of case facts on judicial review. For example, Craig F. Emmert (1992) found that the type of case, the constitutional argument advanced, and the lower court ruling significantly influence state supreme court decisions to invalidate a statute. Susan Fino (1987) also found that when state supreme courts were able to base their decisions on independent state grounds, they were twice as likely to declare the state law unconstitutional.

Evidence from the agenda-setting stage. While Glendon A. Schubert's (1959) research set the stage for strategic accounts of case selection on the nation's highest court, Joseph Tanenhaus and his associates (1963) offered nonstrategic accounts of votes to grant *certiorari* with cue theory. Tanenhaus and his colleagues argued that certain case facts signal judges on whether they should grant or deny review. These "cues" include dissension within the lower court, direct involvement of the federal government, presence of a civil liberty issue, and the presence of an economic issue. According to cue theory, the presence of one or more "cues" explains the court's decision to grant *certiorari*.

Stuart H. Teger and Douglas Kosinski (1980) find support for cue theory overall. However, Teger and Kosinski argue that cue theory does not predict judicial decision making at the agenda-setting stage. Similarly, S. Sidney Ulmer (1972, 1978, 1983) found that conflict with United States Supreme Court precedent explained eight times as much of the variance in the *certiorari* decision compared to the federal government as petitioning party on the Vinson Court and Warren Court (Ulmer 1983). Ulmer (1984) further posited that judges would hear cases when precedent is challenged and when intercircuit conflict exists. Ulmer concluded that the United States Supreme Court is responsive to legal-systemic variables (i.e., conflict) and less governed by the issues of the case.

Despite its normative appeal, many scholars studying judicial decisions have recognized a need to move beyond a legal perspective to incorporate "politics" into explanations of judicial behavior. C. Herman Pritchett (1941) was among the first to raise questions about the utility of a legal approach to judicial behavior. He argued that the approach provided little explanation as to why judges cast particular votes. Moreover, scholars employing integrated and interactive models of judicial behavior have demonstrated that case facts alone do not explain decisions (see, e.g., Brace and Hall 1990, 1997; Segal and Spaeth 1993). Rather scholars have demonstrated that the facts of the case interact with a judge's preference (Rohde and Spaeth 1976; Segal and Spaeth 1993) or institutional rules (Brace and Hall 1990).

Attitudinal Explanations of Judicial Behavior

Another explanation of judicial behavior contends that judicial preferences are the most important predictors of behavior. Scholars working within this framework also have offered a conceptualization of the judiciary that treats courts as independent institutions. Accordingly, judges are not responsive to most or any conditions in their political environments. Instead, judges are beholden to their sincere ideological preferences, which along with case facts shape judicial behavior. This "Attitudinal Model" of judicial behavior has been applied mostly to the United States Supreme Court.

Evidence from the decision-on-the-merits stage. Pritchett (1941) observed over fifty years ago that preferences of the majority on the bench are reflected in what becomes law. Since Pritchett's pioneering study, scholars have employed a variety of approaches to assess the ideological proclivities of judges. These surrogates have been used to tests hypotheses about the relationship between judicial preferences and judicial outcomes. A common approach has been to use justices' votes as a measure of judicial preferences. For example, Schubert (1962 and 1965) applied Guttman scaling to analyze voting behavior on the Warren Court. David W. Rohde and Harold J. Spaeth (1976) applied similar scaling techniques to examine the ideology of United States Supreme Court justices who served on the bench during 1958 through 1973. Similarly, Lawrence Baum (1985) employed an ideological scalogram to classify judges' voting behavior along liberal and conservative lines. Overall, this body of literature demonstrates that preferences shape behavior, particularly on the United States Supreme Court.

Scholars also have used judge partisan affiliation as a "second best measure of preferences" (Kilwein and Brisbin 1997, 138). Some earlier studies found party identification to be an important indicator of judicial voting behavior. For example, Ulmer's (1962) examination of the Michigan Supreme Court and Vines (1964) examination of desegregation found that judicial behavior was largely determined by party identification and region (but see Feeley, 1971; Giles and Walker 1975). Beverly B. Cook's (1973) examination of the determinants of judicial behavior of federal judges when sentencing draft violators also demonstrated that party affiliation influenced sentence severity.

Later, C. Neal Tate (1981) argued that "who the judges are" explains judicial decision making.[4] Tate showed that justices' party affiliation accounted for much of the variation in votes on civil liberty and economic cases before the United States Supreme Court. C. Neal Tate and Roger Handberg (1991) further demonstrated that background variables (i.e., party, religion, class, and experience) retained predictive power when examined across different time periods; however, the influence of background characteristics is context-dependent. Donald R. Songer and Sue Davis (1990) also found party identification significantly explained federal appellate court behavior. Moreover, C. K. Rowland, Donald R. Songer, and Robert A. Carp (1988) found the party affiliation of the president helped determine how judges decided cases.

In an effort to overcome some of the limitations of previous measures of judge preferences (see, e.g., Epstein and Mershon 1996); Jeffrey A. Segal and Albert D. Cover (1989) estimate judge ideology by employing content analysis of newspaper editorials for United States Supreme Court justice nominees.[5] Using this measure of preferences, Segal and Spaeth have provided overwhelming evidence that Supreme Court decisions reflect the ideological preferences of its members (Segal and Spaeth 1993, 69–72; Spaeth and Segal 1999).[6]

Evidence from the agenda-setting stage. Scholars also have found strong support for an attitudinal account of judicial behavior when applied to the agenda-setting stage. Lawrence Baum (1977) for example, examined the criteria by which California Supreme Court judges selected cases for review; he found policy goals were central to these decisions. Baum (1979) also examined whether a vote to hear a case and a vote on the merits were governed by the same constellation of forces. His examination of the two stages of decision making on the California Supreme Court during the 1970–74 period led him to the conclusion that, " . . . decisions on whether to accept cases for hearing in the California Supreme Court are related to decisions on the merits of accepted cases in a substantial way" (1979, 114–15).

Rathjen and Spaeth (1979, 1990) also considered the role of preferences on agenda-setting. They addressed whether or not denial of court access produced a liberal or conservative outcome at the merits stage of the process. Rathjen and Spaeth (1990) demonstrated that judges voted on whether or not they should decide the substantive merits of the controversy according to their ideological preferences; "Denial of access produced conservative effects, which effects correlated extremely highly with the individual justice's ideological preferences" (40).

Emerging from this research is perhaps one of the most enduring findings in judicial politics: ideological preferences of judges influence judicial behavior. Preferences of individual judges therefore are paramount to an understanding of judicial behavior, especially on the United States Supreme Court. Presumably, the United States Supreme Court's insularity allows justices to vote in accordance with their sincere preferences on issues regarding public policy. The institutional autonomy afforded the United States Supreme Court by rules, procedures, and norms, and the stability of the institutional design have preserved this preference-driven explanation of judicial decision making for over five decades.

Neo-Institutional Explanations of Judicial Behavior

Whether judges vote in accordance with their ideological preferences or whether judges alter behavior in response to rules, context, or design, is a fundamental question that scholars continue to debate. Some scholars have examined a constellation of contextual, institutional, and attitudinal factors, embracing a rational choice framework (see, e.g., Brace and Hall 1997). These latter neo-institutional approaches have found evidence of both endogenous (e.g., judge preferences) and exogenous (e.g., method of selection, intermediate appellate court) explanations of judicial behavior. In combination, political scientists working within this framework have demonstrated that courts are responsive institutions whose behavior is often conditioned by institutional rules and designs.

Evidence from the decision-on-the-merits stage. The idea that institutional rules and structure shape judicial behavior or that judges are strategic actors is not new. Rohde and Spaeth (1976) maintain that United States Supreme Court's decisions result from interactions of goals (i.e., the individual and collective attitudes of the members of the Court) and rules (i.e., formal procedures, norms, and rule structures of the institution), which affect individual decision making by enhancing or retarding the process. Other research has demonstrated how rules and norms have shaped opinion assignments on the United States Supreme Court by inducing strategic behavior among members of the Court (see, e.g., Rohde 1972).

Scholars also have examined how intermediate appellate courts might influence judicial behavior on state courts of last resort (Brace and Hall 1990; Hall and Brace 1989; Glick and Pruet 1986; Tarr and Porter 1988). For example, Henry R. Glick and George W. Pruet (1986) find that states with an intermediate appellate court have higher levels of dissent. Melinda Gann Hall and Paul Brace (1989) also find that states with an intermediate appellate court are associated with higher levels of dissent on death penalty cases.

Also, at the state supreme court level, institutional procedures such as order of discussion (Hall and Brace 1989, 1992) and opinion assignment (Hall and Brace 1989, 1992; Brace and Hall 1990) have been posited as important forces shaping judicial behavior. The crux of the argument is that the absence of rules permitting the application of rewards and sanctions facilitates competitive bargaining, thereby increasing dissent.

Brace and Hall (1993) and Hall (1992) also considered the conditioning effect of selection methods on judicial behavior. They found that justices behaved differently when faced with the possibility of electoral sanctions or when they have been exposed to a more partisan process of recruitment. Hall (1987, 1992, 1995) has demonstrated that while voters in judicial elections are generally uninformed, justices nonetheless believe that citizens are aware of some of their decisions. Most fundamentally, elected judges altered their behavior when deciding controversial cases.[7]

Evidence from the agenda-setting stage. Glendon Schubert (1959) first asked if judges strategize when voting on grants of *certiorari* on the United States Supreme Court.[8] Schubert assumed judges would adopt the agenda-setting strategy that would best secure judges' preferred outcomes in the decision-on-the-merits stage. Schubert examined United States Supreme Court justices' votes on federal employees' liability evidentiary cases for the 1942 through 1947 terms. He found that liberal judges seemed to alter their behavior with respect to their perceived notion of the outcome.

Using Justice Harold H. Burton's conference reports, Saul Brenner (1979) examined the actual vote on *certiorari* and decision-on-the-merits stage for judges on the United States Supreme Court during the 1945 through 1957 terms. He posited that judges are rational actors who calculate the possible costs and benefits of their *certiorari* decision prior to casting the vote. Brenner found judges seemingly recognized greater payoffs when they wanted to affirm the lower court decision than when judges wanted to reverse the decision. Judges in the latter category needed to pay closer attention to the probability that their preferred outcome would prevail. His research demonstrates judges behave strategically vis-à-vis the preferences or likely actions of their colleagues.[9]

Jan Palmer's (1982) study is one of the most sophisticated econometric analyses of the agenda-setting process. Palmer explored the relationship between a judge's vote to grant writ of *certiorari* and his/her vote on the merits of the case. Like Schubert and Brenner, Palmer argued that judges are rational actors who calculate the risks, costs, and benefits associated with a decision to grant *certiorari*. Quite simply, judges calculated the expected utility associated with the likely outcome of the decision-on-the-merits stage. These results provide some support for Baum (1977, 1979); Ulmer (1983, 1984); and Brenner (1979); however, Palmer's findings contradict Doris Marie Provine (1980), who found no relationship between vote to grant *certiorari* and the decision-on-the-merits.

Most recently, Robert Boucher and Jeffrey A. Segal (1995) employed multivariate analysis to examine whether judges engage in strategic behavior when "deciding to decide" the case. They overcome previous shortcomings by testing for both aggressive grants and defensive denials (Perry 1991). Boucher and Segal found that, "voting to grant [*certiorari*] is indeed an indicator of the vote on the merits" (1995, 836). Their results supported Brenner's original contention that judges who wish to affirm are more conscious of the costs involved. They also found evidence for aggressive grants, but not for defensive denials. In conclusion, Boucher and Segal "label justices on the Vinson Court neither strategic nor nonstrategic but rather semistrategic" (1995, 836).

This conceptualization provides evidence that judges are responsive to institutional rules, contextual characteristics, electoral and personal preferences, lower appellate courts, and to their brethren at different stages of the judicial process.[10] However, with few exceptions, the literature discussed has followed closely the tradition of examining the judicial branch of government in isolation from the legislative and executive branches of government. As a result, we know very little about the relationship among the judiciary, legislative, and executive branches during both agenda-setting stages and the decision-on-the-merits stages.

It is my contention that treating courts in isolation provides an incomplete understanding of the role of courts as policymaking (and unmaking) institutions. Political scientists have long been interested in the relationships between Congress and the presidency in terms of policymaking (see, e.g., Wildvasky 1966; Rivers and Rose 1985; Bond and Fleisher 1990; Brace and Hinkley 1992); a natural progression seems to warrant the inclusion of the judiciary. Without systematic comparative examinations of courts in relation to other branches of government, our understanding of the degree to which the system of checks and balances shapes judicial behavior, and subsequently public policy, is limited. Perhaps most importantly, the conditions under which courts are independent actors capable and willing to impose their preferences on policy through the power of judicial review remain elusive. Progress in this arena has been hampered by sparse and disjointed findings. Data limitations also have thwarted progress in this area.

Separation-of-Powers Games as Explanations of Judicial Behavior

According to some accounts in positive theory, the preferences of other branches of government are expected to constrain judicial behavior (see, e.g., Ferejohn and Shipan 1990; Eskridge 1991; Gely and Spiller 1990, 1992; Epstein and Walker 1995; Langer, 1997; Epstein and Knight, 1998). The central issue underlying this conceptualization of judicial review is whether or not justices are induced to vote strategically vis-à-vis other political institutions (Murphy 1964).

A definition of strategic behavior is borrowed from Kenneth A. Shepsle and Mark A. Bonchek's (1997) recent account of rational choice approaches to studying courts: "[S]trategic behavior, in short, taking the full horizon of a process into account, may require individuals to make seemingly less-than-ideal choices at some points in order to secure superior outcomes at the end of the trail" (1997, 151). In other words, strategic behavior is not merely a one-shot, myopic decision, but rather one that considers a long sequence of

choices in an iterative process. Judges thus should vote prospectively according to the anticipated reactions from the other branches of government. This
type of strategic behavior should manifest in judicial voting behavior when
justices alter decisions in response to preferences of other branches of government as well as the conditions in their environment that make judges more
vulnerable to retaliation.

Evidence from the decision-on-the-merits stage. Walter Murphy (1964) was
among the first to view judges as rational actors who calculate their decisions
based on the anticipated actions of Congress. Brian Marks (1989) was the
first to apply the separation-of-powers game to the Court. Since Marks'
project, scholars working within this framework have argued that the Court
will alter its behavior in response to the expected retaliation from other political actors, namely, Congress.

William N. Eskridge (1991) posited a sequential game of interaction
among the Court, Congress, and the president, focusing on congressional
overrides of federal statutory decisions from 1967–90. In this study, Eskridge
examined the extent to which Congress overrides Court decisions and under
what conditions. He argued that members of Congress were aware of the
Court's statutory decisions and that each actor devoted significant efforts
toward analyzing the policy implications. Fundamentally, Eskridge found that
Congress was most likely to override the United States Supreme Court's
decision when the Court's decision revealed an ideologically fragmented court.

Rafael Gely and Pablo T. Spiller (1990, 1992) and Spiller and Gely
(1992) also suggested that the Court acquiesces to Congress when confronted with a threatening political environment or the possibility of seeing
their most preferred policy rejected in favor of their least preferred outcome.
Gely and Spiller (1992) developed a formal model of strategic behavior by
United States Supreme Court justices with respect to constitutional cases.
When ideal preference points of three legislative bodies (i.e., Congress, president, and state legislatures) were far from each other, Gely and Spiller found
that the set of feasible constitutional outcomes was larger.[11] Specifically, they
examined two United States Supreme Court decisions: *West Coast Hotel Co.
v. Parrish* 300 U.S. 379 (1937), a decision that upheld a state minimum
wage law, and *National Labor Relations Board v. Jones and Laughlin Steel Corp*
301 U.S. 1 (1937), which imposed controls over labor-management relations
in industry. In both cases, Justice Owen J. Robert's vote was decisive in
upholding these statutes. Prior to these cases, the statutes in question had
not been upheld.

Gely and Spiller contend that Franklin Delano Roosevelt's announce-
ment of the court-packing plan was neither the only nor the primary reason
for the "switch in time to save nine." Rather, they posited that election results

exaggerated the Court's fears. The elections of 1936 secured tremendous gains for the Democrats, giving them control of Congress and thirty-three state legislatures. As a result, the political environment confronting the Court was conducive to an override via constitutional amendment; Congress now had the necessary support. Spiller and Gely concluded, "only when Congress and the state legislatures are divided does the preferences of the justices matter in interpreting the Constitution" (1992, 65).

Following their case-study approach, Spiller and Gely (1992) also developed a formal model for nonconstitutional decisions. In this study, they empirically tested the hypotheses derived from their formal model. Spiller and Gely analyzed United States Supreme Court decisions in national labor relations cases and found evidence that the Court often was constrained by congressional preferences. Fundamentally, they concluded that the United States Supreme Courts is a strategic actor that responds to threatening external political stimuli (see also Epstein and Walker 1995; Epstein and Knight 1998).[12]

Evidence from the agenda-setting stage. Utilizing a comparative approach to study strategic behavior in state supreme courts, Paul Brace, Melinda Gann Hall, and Laura Langer (1999) were first to provide preliminary evidence that separation-of-powers explanations apply to American state supreme courts under some conditions (see also Langer 1997; Brace, Hall, and Langer 2001). They found that the likelihood of a docketed case resolving a constitutional challenge to abortion laws varies predictably with the conditions in court environments. Specifically, divided government, judicial selection method, discretionary docket, the constitutional provision for right to privacy, and length of a justice's term significantly influence the likelihood that courts will review statutes. Similarly, Brace, Hall, and Langer found that votes to invalidate state statutes were less likely to occur on elected courts, but more likely to occur on courts with life tenure and under divided government.

Linkages between judicial outcomes and the preferences of each branch of government are the foci of many scholarly debates. A separation-of-powers approach to study judicial review focuses attention on when the judiciary is most likely to diverge from the preferences of other governmental actors and what consequences this has on public policy and democratic institutions. This approach also reinforces the need to bring institutional rules, political context, and the distribution of preferences to the forefront of judicial behavior. Moreover, the approach facilitates a deeper understanding of interrelationships among all branches of government. In this way, separation-of-powers models can be viewed as an extension of the neo-institutional and political contextual approaches, positing very specific external influences. These external forces have formal government authority and constitute the actors involved in constitutional systems of checks and balances.

MOTIVATIONS OF JUDGES

As scholars continue to seek answers to what explains judicial behavior, the acceptance of one conceptualization and the refutation of others will continue to be debated. Central to this debate are concerns with both the nature of institutional autonomy afforded the judiciary and the nature of the threat posed by other branches of government. Clearly, it is difficult to address these issues when focusing on a single set of institutional arrangements. It might be that separation-of-powers games do emerge, but not with courts as insular as the United States Supreme Court.

The predominant literature on judicial strategic behavior does not consider electoral motivations of judges; strategic behavior is defined in terms of policy retaliation. This manifestation of strategic behavior might be appropriate for studying behavior on the United States Supreme Court; however, such a narrow definition of strategic behavior does not serve us well when studying courts where judges also pursue electoral goals.

Varying conceptualizations of the judiciary could be attributable to fundamental differences in the institution being analyzed. Much of this literature has focused on a single court where institutional rules, constitutional design, and political settings rarely change. It is the premise of this book that institutional rules, constitutional designs, and strategic settings, induce some state supreme court justices to pay attention to both policy and electoral threats imposed by other branches of government. Other settings encourage justices to challenge the preferences of other branches of government.

The American states provide an opportunity to examine judicial behavior in a comparative setting. Paul Brace and Aubrey Jewett (1995) observed recently, "[a] majority of the energy in the American politics subfield goes to studying single institutions, and our understanding of institutions such as Congress and the Supreme Court has advanced. Yet this approach has obvious limitations if we are ever to arrive at truly general theories of political processes that are not bound by time or place. As Michael Mezey (1993) observed, 'a theory of a single institution is like having a theory of relativity that only applies to Chicago'" (665). Certainly, letting institutional rules, constitutional designs, and political settings vary could help us understand more completely judicial behavior.

Another reason there is little consensus over what explains judicial behavior is that we have not spent enough time examining the impact agenda-setting has on the decision-on-the-merits. Modeling the dynamics of both stages provides a holistic view of the judicial process and advances our conceptualization of courts. Factors that influence one stage might not be important in the other stage. Studying one stage in isolation therefore can easily contribute to mixed conceptualizations of the judiciary and inaccurate empirical analysis.

Inconsistent findings and divergent conceptualizations of the judiciary also might be due to idiosyncrasies of single cases, types of case, or areas of law. With few exceptions, scholars have focused on judicial behavior with respect to nonconstitutional cases (e.g., statutory interpretation) or on the behavior of judges in a single case or single area of law. An examination of judicial behavior in constitutional cases across different areas of law is necessary if we want to gain a more complete understanding of the role of courts in the policymaking and unmaking process. After all, judicial review enhances the adversarial relationship between judges and the other branches of government. Moreover, judicial review is one of the most obvious ways judges make policy.

One goal of this book is to advance a more general theory of judicial behavior. To do so, attention must focus on systematic comparisons of courts that operate under a variety of institutional rules, designs, and settings; yet we must compare courts that are comparable enough so we can make accurate and reliable inferences. Thus, exploring further various conceptualizations of judicial behavior, this project addresses whether or not, and under what conditions, state supreme court justices vote according to their own ideology or if judicial votes to review and invalidate state laws are influenced by legislative and gubernatorial threats? Most fundamentally, I ask if existing explanations of judicial behavior can be generalized across policy areas, across both stages of judicial review, and across courts with varying degrees of autonomy.

Chapter Three

A Theory of State Supreme Court Judicial Review

WHAT MOTIVATES RETALIATION?

Why do legislatures and governors care what members of state supreme courts do and what, if anything, can they do about it? Judges can reinterpret or invalidate legislation and the other branches can respond to judicial behavior by overriding judicial decisions. Legislatures and governors also can return an adverse retention vote to penalize judges for objectionable decisions. A brief glance at the motivations of other branches of government can shed light on why legislators and governors would expend energy to retaliate against judges.

From the nation's inception, scholars have recognized the political ambitions of politicians (e.g., career and policy goals) and how institutional designs and structures might frustrate or promote these ambitions. According to Joseph A. Schlesinger (1966, 1991) the source of such political ambitions can be dated to James Madison, who in *The Federalist* papers, no. 51, explained how "the separation of powers, by allowing ambition to 'counteract ambition' will make the proposed constitution effective" (1991, 35).

Decades ago, scholars taking an economic, rational approach to studying democratic institutions and governmental actors argued that the competitive pursuit of ambition (whether electoral or policy) was the quintessential tenet of the institutional design of American politics. According to Joseph A. Schumpeter (1942), a democracy can be defined as "that institutional arrangement for arriving at political decisions in which individuals acquire the power to decide by means of a competitive struggle for the people's vote" (1942, 269). The work of Anthony Downs (1957) also indicates electoral and policy goals shape behavior, particularly among political parties. He posited that the primary goal of parties was to win control of office. In that pursuit, parties were viewed as rational actors, altering their behavior to reach that goal (Downs 1957, 25).

Schlesinger (1966, 1991) posited that most officeholders have ambitions associated with policy or career goals. Career goals (i.e., electoral goals) involve retaining the current office or aspiring to hold an office more prestigious than the one currently occupied. Schlesinger argued that such ambition affects the decisions of policyholders; "the constituency to which the legislator is responding is not always the one from which he has been elected because they often seek higher offices" (1991, 36).

Congressional scholars following the lead of Richard F. Fenno (1973, 1978) have argued that members of Congress are motivated primarily by reelection goals (Mayhew 1974; Arnold 1990).[1] David R. Mayhew's (1974) description of legislators as "single-minded reelection seekers" is perhaps most notable (1974, 17). Closely tied to the reelection bid is the need for members to pay close attention to their constituents. Fenno (1978) noted that there is a general sense in Congress that if you "stray too far from your district you'll lose it." Research by Bruce Cain, John Ferejohn, and Morris Fiorina (1987) also has shown indirect linkages exist between constituency preferences and voting behavior. Other studies have shown fear of potential challengers contributes to ideological congruence between representative and constituent (Arnold 1990). Similarly, students studying the executive branch have demonstrated that presidents also are rational actors motivated by policy and electoral goals (e.g., Brace and Hinkley 1992; Moe 1993; Sinclair 1993; Cohen 1997).

Clearly members of the legislative and executive branches pursue electoral and policy goals, among others. When a justice imposes his/her preferences on public policy, he/she interferes with the ability of government actors to pursue their goals. The very act of voting to review and invalidate a statute can restrict the domain of feasible policy alternatives from which the legislative and executive branches select in the future. This narrower domain of feasible alternatives hinders ambitions. Even if the court's outcome upholds the legislation, a single vote to invalidate the statute nonetheless restricts the domain of feasible policy alternatives, especially when the judge who voted to strike down the law writes a separate opinion.

For these reasons, legislators and governors often view state supreme court justices as distant relatives not welcome in the policy arena. Harold J. Spaeth observed that the characteristics of the American constitutional system allow judges, particularly United States Supreme Court justices, to function "not merely as policy makers who are adjuncts to legislators, executives, and administrators, but as the most authoritative of our society's allocators of resources" (1979, 1). More recently, Kenneth A. Shepsle and Mark S. Bonchek

(1997) argued that it is useful to conceptualize judges as "legislators in robes" because just like members of Congress, judges pursue policy goals (1997, 450). Such policy pronouncements from any member on the bench are typically frowned upon in most legislatures, especially when it involves an important issue or a fiscal matter. Legislatures view policymaking and the power of the purse in their domain.

Separation-of-powers creates a competitive relationship in which members of each branch of government are expected to invoke their check when the actions of the other are seen as threatening or unorthodox. Judicial review also might be threatening to the legislature and governor because these actors see judicial review as an encroachment of power. In short, judges have reasons to worry about future actions by the legislative and executive branches, and vice versa.

LEGISLATIVE-JUDICIAL RELATIONS: A TIT-FOR-TAT GAME

Anecdotal evidence indicates that state legislatures worry about reversals and judges worry about legislative retaliation. For example, House Speaker Daniel Blue of North Carolina observed that the complexity of issues for which state governments are responsible require greater communication between the legislature and judiciary (Blue, 1991, 31). Blue describes the North Carolina legislature as one that has ongoing discussions with members of the state supreme court, especially before the legislature enacts legislation. Discussions between governmental branches, as well as legislative history, advisory opinions, and the like, provide cues to judges about legislative and gubernatorial preferences and the likelihood of retaliation. Similarly, court rulings and court ideology help guide legislatures when enacting policy (Brace and Langer 2001; Rogers 2001).

Often state supreme court justices reference the legislative history pertaining to the challenged law. For example, in one of the cases examined in this book, a New Hampshire state supreme court justice noted in his opinion that legislative history clearly indicated that the workers' compensation law in question was enacted in direct response to previous court cases. This justice further noted that the sponsor of the legislation intended to clarify the language of previous laws in response to two other New Hampshire Supreme Court opinions (*Estabrook v American Hoist & Derrick, Inc.*, 127 NH 162, 165). Such language is common in these opinions. Here judges seemingly recognize that the legislature might be trying to accommodate judges and avoid further legislative reversals.

In a similar workers' compensation case, the Supreme Court of New Hampshire noted in its majority opinion that the legislature had amended the law in question four times in response to court rulings, including the *Estabrook* decision. After several iterations, the Supreme Court of New Hampshire was asked again in *Young v Prevue Products Inc.*, 130 NH, 84, (1987), about the constitutionality of the amended "exclusivity of remedy" clause of the workers' compensation statute. This time, the New Hampshire Supreme Court over-ruled their *Estabrook* decision and declared the statutory provision constitutional.

In another case involving campaign and election laws, the Pennsylvania Supreme Court invalidated a provision of Pennsylvania Election Code, which imposed criminal sanctions on candidates for public office who publish po-litical advertisements about opponents without giving opponents prior con-tent notification. The justices noted in their opinion that the legislature adopted the 1972 statute following the Pennsylvania Supreme Court's invalidation of Article I, Section 7 of the Pennsylvania Constitution.[2]

The California court of last resort provides more anecdotal evidence of tit-for-tat games legislatures and judges often play. In *County of San Mateo v Boss* 479 P. 2d 654 (1971), the California Supreme Court concluded that children of a parent who had received public assistance from the state were not responsible for supporting the parent(s) as per section 206 of the Cali-fornia Civil Code (3 Cal.3d 962). In the majority opinion, the California Supreme Court concluded that because the provisions in question created a duty for children of any "*poor* person" to maintain such person to the extent of their ability, Boss, the adult son, was not required to pay; his mother was "in need" but not poor.

Following this decision, the California legislature amended the provision as part of the Welfare Reform Act of 1971. The reversed section 206 of the California Civil Code essentially replaced the words "*poor* person" with the statement, "any person *in need*." When this provision was challenged two years later in *Swoap v Superior Court of Sacramento County*, 516 P.2d 840 the California Supreme Court noted in the majority opinion that the legislature was responding to the *Boss* decision. The California Supreme Court found the amended section constitutional.

Another case in Wyoming further illustrates informational exchanges between the legislative and judicial branches and the concern about retalia-tion. The Wyoming Supreme Court's majority opinion in *Mills v Reynolds* (837 P.2d 48; 1992) stated that if the legislature were to identify a compelling state interest, the court would likely permit the inclusion of "complete immu-nity clauses for co-employees" in workers' compensation legislation. Because no compelling reason was given, the court invalidated that provision of the statute. Presumably in an effort to appease the legislature (or avoid legislative retaliation) the Wyoming Supreme Court hinted twice in its opinion that future interactions between this court and the legislature might be more favorable to the legislature.

In *Mitchell v Steffen* 504 N.W.2d 198 (1993), the Supreme Court of Minnesota demonstrated the power of judicial review on budgetary matters confronting legislatures. The Supreme Court of Minnesota declared unconstitutional a Minnesota statute passed in 1991, which imposed residency requirements on recipients of General Assistance Work Readiness Benefits. The Minnesota Supreme Court concluded that the statute burdened citizens' fundamental right to travel and violated the Equal Protection Clause of the U.S. Constitution. In the majority opinion, the justices noted that the state legislature had passed the law in response to a budget crisis, but essentially the justices argued that their hands were tied to protect the rights of citizens.

Clearly these examples indicate that justices are concerned about retaliation and that each branch of government pays attention to the policy preferences of the others. Moreover, these examples reveal judicial review as an iterative process. However, in the illustrations above, justices observed legislative attempts to comply with court rulings and wrote the majority opinion in a way that might dissuade anticipated legislative retaliatory action.

In other cases, legislative history reveals state supreme court justices are less concerned about retaliation, especially when state legislatures act in defiance of court rulings. For example, in one election case examined, the Connecticut Supreme Court noted in its majority opinion that the legislature had amended provisions of *The Campaign Financing Act* in response to a ruling by the Connecticut Supreme Court. However, the justices further noted that the amended provisions were not the portions of the law that this court had previously declared unconstitutional (*State v Proto*; 526 A.2d 1297 (1987). The legislature left the declared unconstitutional provisions intact. The language used by the justices in this case revealed a sense of hostility toward the legislature, which in the court's eyes blatantly disregarded the court's previous ruling. The Connecticut Supreme Court declared the provisions unconstitutional, sending a warning to the legislature.

Legislative histories and court opinions are commonly referenced to dissuade retaliatory actions, facilitate judicial-legislative cooperation, or convey a warning to members of the other branches. Many American states also have formalized communication mechanisms between legislatures and state supreme courts (Hunzeker 1990). Use of judicial advisory opinions is one formalized mechanism that is often indicative of strategic calculations. State legislatures employ judicial advisory opinions to ask state supreme court justices whether or not a prospective bill would pass constitutional muster. Such instances are not uncommon in the American states, illustrating legislative awareness of judicial behavior and the power of judicial review.

According to the National Conference on State Courts (NCSC), these formal judicial advisory opinions on legislation are used regularly in at least eleven states. While court answers in these instances are neither definitive nor binding, they nonetheless give legislatures a "heads up" on how judges might vote. Advisory opinions also provide some indication of legislative preferences to the members on the bench, preparing them for future interactions with other governmental branches.

For example, the Supreme Judicial Court of Massachusetts in 1971 was asked about the constitutionality of a proposed bill that restricted eligibility for public assistance. The proposed legislation would require that applicants reside in the Commonwealth for one year prior to receiving any benefits. While the bill did not pass at this time, a one-year residency requirement for public aid applicants would provide additional opportunities for the Supreme Judicial Court of Massachusetts to rule on this issue. Many other state courts of last resort also have been asked similar questions by either the legislature or the governor.

State judiciary addresses are another indication that legislatures and courts pay attention to one another. Thirty-three states use state of the judiciary addresses to facilitate legislative-judicial relations according to the NCSC. Additionally, the National Conference of State Legislatures (NCSL) noted that more than half of the states have a staff person in the judiciary to serve as liaison with legislative and executive branches (Hunzeker 1990). Formal communications among governmental branches is not a necessity for strategic behavior to occur, because all fifty states have formal separation-of-powers and systems of checks and balances. As a result of these checks and balances, policy threats are quite common and expected.

Besides fear of policy retaliation, justices also fear electoral retaliation. In 1990, NCSL conducted a survey on judicial-legislative relations; some of the findings indicate that judges indeed perceive their votes to be at risk. Donna Hunzeker, a senior policy specialist at NCSL observed, "[t]he involvement of state judges in the policy process is thought by some observers to be a natural consequence of the fact that more than half of them are elected and most others, while initially appointed, must later be retained. . . ." (1990, 1). Hunzeker also noted that,"[f]or the judiciary, the sorest spot in legislative-judicial relations may be when legislative appropriations for court operations and judicial salaries, or decisions about judicial selection are perceived as being used to retaliate against unpopular decisions. . . ." (1990; 1)

A few more examples of legislative/gubernatorial threats to judges' careers are informative. Recently, Chief Justice David Brock of New Hampshire was engaged in a battle with the governor and legislature over a controversial ruling in a school funding case. The politicians were calling for Brock's impeachment, but it failed. Similarly, in 1994, the chief justice of the Rhode Island Supreme Court resigned rather than face impeachment. Policy differences between the chief justice and other branches of government also contributed in this instance to the call for his removal.

These exchanges heightened animosity between state supreme court justices and state legislatures and governors.

The reelection of South Carolina's Supreme Court Justice Jean Toal provides another example of the intense politics surrounding legislative and gubernatorial reelection/reappointment of these judges. In a very close, politicized vote, Justice Toal was painted as a liberal activist and subjected to fierce opposition when her term expired in 1996; the legislature had the authority to vote her in or out. Despite the close call and opposition, her term was renewed and she was subsequently installed as Chief Justice for one Supreme Court of South Carolina on March 23, 2000.

The threat of losing her seat was very real. Central to the debate was Toal's record and willingness to vote out-of-sync with the state legislature, and governor in particular.

These examples are quite illustrative of the electoral threats imposed by the legislature and governor and the seriousness with which state supreme court justices view these threats. The examples above also demonstrate the adversarial relationship between judges and the other branches of government often sparked by judicial review.[3] Finally, they highlight the need to understand these relationships among justices and other governmental actors and the consequences of these relations on judicial review. Clearly, judges are viewed as pivotal participants in the policymaking arena.

Like other politicians, judges are concerned when their electoral or policy goals are threatened. As rational actors, judges play a sequential game of anticipated action with the legislature and governor. These nested games, according to George Tsebelis (1990) suggest that, "the actor may choose a suboptimal strategy in one game if this strategy happens to maximize his payoffs when all arenas are taken into account" (1990, 9).[4]

DEFINING A JUDGE'S SAFETY ZONE AND EXPECTED RETALIATORY THREATS

Justices are assumed to be rational actors who seek to maximize goals. In this way, the research builds from Walter Murphy's (1964) concept of judicial behavior based on a rational calculation of self-interest (see also Rohde and Spaeth 1976). However, in these studies, scholars examined the behavior of United States Supreme Court justices as rational actors in pursuit of policy goals. These unique actors are unlike most politicians; the typical politician (and judge) often pursues multiple goals simultaneously as a result of institutional rules and design. Thus, in the American states, supreme court justices are assumed to be rational actors who pursue at least two goals: (1) translating their sincere preferences into public policy, and (2) retaining their seat on the bench.

The assumption that some state supreme court justices also pursue electoral goals is consistent with neo-institutional approaches that have been employed to study judicial dissent (Brace and Hall 1990; Brace and Hall 1995; Brace and Hall 1997), and judicial review (Brace, Hall, and Langer 1999) in state supreme courts.

A second important assumption, also consistent with positive theory, is that when state justices exercise their power of judicial review, they knowingly risk electoral or policy retaliation for their actions. Institutional rules and political contexts, which vary substantially across the fifty states, are expected to condition the extent to which these threats are realized in important ways.

A third assumption, consistent with separation-of-powers games, is that justices have some information regarding the preferences of the legislature and governor. Knowledge about the preferences of these actors presumably allows justices to calculate the degree of risk associated with their actions. Finally, I assume that there are legislative/gubernatorial costs associated with policy and electoral retaliation against a justice. This assumption is also consistent with positive political theorist accounts of judicial behavior (see, e.g., Segal 1997; but see Eskridge 1991).

From a theoretical perspective, state government is expected to incur costs when government retaliates against a judge for his/her decisions.[5] As a result, there is a range of feasible alternatives acceptable to the legislature and governor. This range of feasible alternatives is called the "Judge's safety zone" (JSZ). If the judge's decision were to fall within that zone, the state legislature and governor are not expected to retaliate against the judge because it is not worth fighting over. The expected utility from such action does not outweigh the cost. In other words, the judge acts as if his/her decision is insolated from political pressures, namely, the legislature and governor.

Baseline maximum and minimum reservation points and ideal preference points define each safety zone. The areas to the right and left of these points refer to the zone of expected retaliatory action (see fig. 3.1). In these instances, the utility associated with accepting the judge's decision does not outweigh the costs of retaliation; state government is thus expected to retaliate.

As noted earlier, state government can reenact statutes, amend the constitution and/or remove justices from the bench. The existence of these sanctions is defined by institutional rules, constitutional designs, and political settings. The intensity of these threats is expected to vary across policy areas. Thus, the political environment defines the size of the safety zone and the issue before the judge heightens (or weakens) the importance of a judge's environment. The size of the safety zone indicates the degree to which judges are free from retaliation.

In this book, I explore five political conditions across four areas of law that are expected to contract or expand the safety zone and influence votes

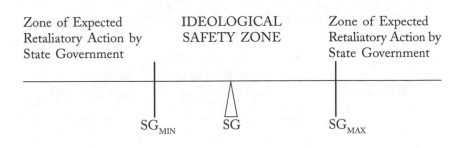

Fig. 3.1. Conceptualizing a Judge's Safety Zone

Where SG = Ideal preference point of state government; SG_{MIN} = state governments' minimum reservation point; SG_{MAX} = state government's maximum reservation point.

in judicial review cases: (1) judge preferences relative to the legislature and governor (i.e., ideological distance), (2) divided control of government, (3) difficulty of constitutional amendment, (4) length of judicial terms, and (5) method of judicial retention.

Most fundamentally, adjustments to the safety zone are expected to differ across areas of law with varying degrees of saliency. These adjustments translate into expansion or contraction of the judge's safety zone according to fear of policy and electoral sanctions, conditioned by the saliency of the policy area. The general idea builds upon separation-of-powers formal models (e.g., Spiller and Gely 1992) and empirical specifications (e.g., Segal 1997). Figure 3.2 illustrates how these factors can make adjustments to the baseline reservation points, expanding or contracting the safety zone (AB_{MIN} and AB_{MAX} in fig. 3.2).

Fear of Policy Retaliation as Constraints on Justices

Recall that the rules and conditions in the political environment define the safety zone. The likelihood that state government will sanction a justice increases when the benefit from retaliation outweighs the cost. Thus, when it is easier to punish a judge, the likelihood of retaliation is greater and consequently the safety zone is narrow (i.e., contracts). Under these conditions a judge is expected to refrain from reviewing constitutional challenges to a state statute. Three mechanisms of policy retaliation are considered. Under these conditions a judge is expected to alter his/her behavior in response to the anticipated policy reactions of the legislature and governor.

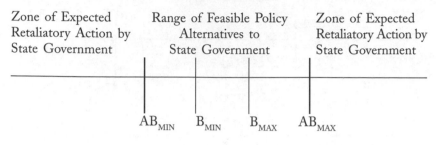

INSTITUTIONAL/CONTEXTUAL
SAFETY ZONE

Zone of Expected Retaliatory Action by State Government	Range of Feasible Policy Alternatives to State Government	Zone of Expected Retaliatory Action by State Government

$$AB_{MIN} \qquad B_{MIN} \qquad B_{MAX} \qquad AB_{MAX}$$

Fig. 3.2. Contraction or Expansion of Judge's Safety Zone

Where B_{MIN} and B_{MAX} = the baseline minimum and maximum reservation points for state government, *ceteris paribus*; AB_{MIN} and AB_{MAX} = the adjusted minimum and maximum reservation points.

Ideological distance. A fundamental hypothesis derived from the separation-of-powers models is that distance between a judge's preference and the preferences of other branches of government is expected to result in strategic behavior (see, e.g., Segal 1997). When the preferences of the judge and other branches of government conflict, judges should be more likely to engage in the policymaking process *if* they can do so without fear of policy retaliation. If preferences were the only factor shaping behavior and state supreme court justices were not concerned about policy retaliation, ideological distance would always predict intervention. Presumably, justices view ideological distance as an opportunity to impute their preferences on issues of public policy, absent rules, and political contexts that make policy or electoral retribution more likely.

Figure 3.3 illustrates how ideological distance is expected to influence judicial review. When the justice is within the reservation points of state government there is no constraint (e.g., C_C in fig. 3.3). Under these conditions state supreme court justices are expected to act as if policy retaliation is not a concern. Here the justice's preferences are consonant with the other branches of government. Presumably the justice, if he/she votes for intervention, will vote to legitimate the policies of the current lawmaking body. At the very least, the justice's vote will be acceptable to the legislature and governor.

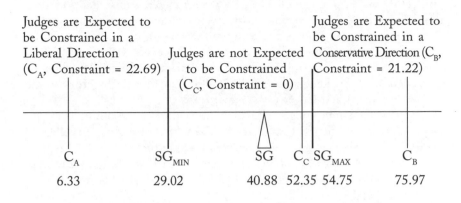

Fig. 3.3. Empirical Measurement of Ideological Distance

Where SG = ideal preference point of state government; SG_{MIN} = state government's minimum reservation point; SG_{MAX} = state government's maximum reservation point; C_A, C_C, and, C_B = estimated ideal preference points for state supreme court justice, outside of safety zone in liberal direction, inside safety zone, and outside safety zone in conservative direction, respectively.

Alternatively, as the justice moves away from the upper or lower reservation points, the constraint operating on the justice is expected to be higher (e.g., C_A and C_B in fig. 3.3).

Ideological distance is reasoned to be one condition under which justices might fear policy retaliation. Recall the discussion about counteracting of ambitions among the three branches of government. When the court intervenes to review a law, the feasible policy alternatives for the legislature and governor are limited, at least in the short run. As a result, the legislature and governor might not be able to appease their constituents. This situation creates a strong incentive for each of the actors to react, particularly when there is ideological distance. Stated differently, when the preferences of the justice diverge from the preferences of state government, judicial intervention in a policy area is threatening to the legislature and governor. The threat weighs more heavily in some areas of law more than other areas of law.

Defining and measuring ideological distance. Measurement of preferences for the actors involved in the policymaking game is critical to assess whether state supreme court justices engage in strategic behavior. Until recently, a satisfactory measure of judge ideology was unavailable, and students of state courts were forced to use judge party identification as a crude surrogate. Recent research has produced a comparable measure of ideology for each state supreme court justice serving on the bench between 1970 and 1993. In this project, I use a contextual based surrogate measure of judicial preferences developed in Brace, Langer and Hall (2000) that correlates highly with the well known Segal and Cover (1989) approach.

Paul Brace, Laura Langer, and Melinda Gann Hall (2000) use the ideology of the appointing government or citizenry to infer justice ideology at the time of initial selection to the bench and weight these scores by the party of the justice. This measure of justice preference has passed extensive validity screening and is much more accurate than simple party identification (Brace, Langer, and Hall 2000).

The preferences of the government also are critical if we wish to assess whether state supreme court justices engage in strategic voting behavior. State scholars have recently provided comparable longitudinal measures of state elite ideology (see Berry, Ringquist, Fording, and Hanson 1998). The annual measure of ideology for the legislature and governor, based on interest-group ratings of members of Congress, provides estimates of the state government's ideal preference point with respect to public policy.[6]

In combination, the preferences of justices and of state government are needed to estimate the degree and direction of the expected constraint on judicial behavior. Three types of preference constraint were estimated for every state supreme court justice (see fig. 3.3).[7] Based on each justice's safety zone, whether or not a justice is constrained is computed. Next, whether or not a justice is constrained in a conservative direction is determined. Finally, liberal constraint is estimated. Hence, the measure of constraint (i.e., ideological distance) is equal to zero when the justice is below the "threshold" or inside the safety zone. When the justice is above the "threshold" or outside the safety zone, constraint equals the difference between the justice's preference point and the upper or lower reservation point.

For illustration, figure 3.3 shows the ideal preference point of the government in Alabama for 1970 (i.e., 40.88). As the justice's ideal preference moves to the left or right of the state government's reservation points, the government is expected to sanction that judge. For example, judges whose ideal preference points fall to the left of state government's minimum reservation point or above the threshold for retaliation are expected to be constrained in a liberal direction (i.e., C_A in fig. 3.3). Alternatively, judges whose ideal preference points fall in the zone to the right of state government's maximum reservation point are expected to be constrained in a conservative direction (i.e., C_B in fig. 3.3). Finally, the figure illustrates a judge whose ideal preference point falls within the safety zone. Judges within the safety zone will not be constrained by the preferences of the government (i.e., C_C in fig. 3.3).

This empirical measure captures the ideological distance between each judge and state government. The greater the distance in preferences, the more likely the actions of the judge will be constrained, particularly in the decision-on-the-merits stage. In short, ideological distance should contract a judge's safety zone.

Divided government. According to positive political theory, viewing judges as participants in the policymaking arena yields another prediction: "the further the distance between Congress and the President, the wider the latitude afforded to the courts" (Weingast 1996, 174). This implies that state supreme court justices have considerable influence during periods of sustained differences between the legislature and governor (e.g., periods of divided government). As a result, divided government can be viewed as another means of adjusting the baselines for the safety zone. More specifically, divided government expands the safety zone giving justices more room to act without fear of policy retaliation.

Amending state constitutions. Besides divided government, there are many institutional procedures that might also impinge on the likelihood of policy retaliation in the states. One consideration in this project is the difficulty in the amendment process. When members of the judiciary intervene in the legislative arena, the legislature can react by overturning the judicial ruling through constitutional amendment. Not only would a constitutional amendment invalidate the justice's decision, it also could hinder future interactions with other branches of government (Spiller and Gely 1992). Fundamentally, justices want to avoid seeing their least preferred outcome become policy, particularly in the form of a constitutional amendment. For these reasons, when it is more difficult for the legislature and governor to amend the constitution, state supreme court justices should be less fearful of policy retaliation, thus expanding their safety zone.

Overturning a decision on constitutional grounds that invalidates a statute is generally more difficult than overturning a decision that interprets a statute. For this reason, critics of separation-of-powers models applied to the United States Supreme Court generally have not considered fear of constitutional amendment as an effective threat operating on judicial behavior. However, state constitutions are considerably easier to amend than the United States Constitution. The difficulty in amending state constitutions varies tremendously across states (Lutz 1994; see also Tarr 1996, 1998; Hammons 1999). Thus, the threat of constitutional revision to overturn a justice's preferred outcome will be greater in the states and will vary across states.

Fear of Electoral Retaliation as Constraints on Judges

As noted before, separation-of-powers models were developed primarily for federal judges with lifetime appointments. At the state level, judges are retained in a variety of ways, creating potential vulnerabilities that could be expected to impinge on their strategic calculations. Thus, equally important are considerations of how these institutional rules shape the safety zone. The crux of the argument is that when institutional rules make electoral retaliation easier for state government, the safety zone contracts and the threat of retaliation looms larger.

If how judges behave on the bench is central to an understanding of the court's role in the policymaking arena, then the rules that determine how judges retain their seats are fundamental. As noted earlier, retention methods afford the actors involved in the process direct opportunities to sanction and reward the members on the bench. Hence, methods of retention can contract or expand a justice's safety zone.

Critical to an understanding of how the linkages between judges and the other branches of government shape judicial behavior is the idea of sanctions and rewards. Over thirty years ago, V. O. Key (1961) in his book *Public Opinion and American Democracy* argued that interest groups, political parties, and elections institutionalize channels of communication between the public and politicians. These channels are expected to serve as mechanisms for the public to influence policy because they provide direct opportunities to reward or punish elected officials for their actions.

We can apply similar logic to the relationship between the judiciary and the other branches of government. We might expect certain rules or political contexts to weaken (or strengthen) the linkages between the branches of government, thereby making each branch less (or more) accountable to the others. Treating the judiciary in isolation thus ignores important dynamics of the policymaking process and seemingly implies that the judiciary is one check that has ultimate authority in the system of checks and balances. Ignoring alternative threats that operate on many judges also adds to the idea that the judicial branch of government has an awesome unchecked power of judicial review.

Significant and predictable behavioral shifts in response to political situations and institutional rules reasoned to heighten or reduce policy and electoral fears indicate strategic behavior. For the purposes of presentation, the general hypotheses are delineated below. The only differences in the specification of the models across each area of law are with respect to control variables, unit effects, and time effects.

EXPECTATIONS ABOUT STAGE I: THE AGENDA-SETTING STAGE

If judges are acting strategically, this behavior certainly should not be limited to the decision-on-the-merits stage. Quite the contrary, some of the greatest opportunities for strategic activity may take place in the agenda-setting stage. As John Kingdon notes: "It is important to keep in mind that in the process of setting the agenda and specifying the alternatives, a good many policy options are eliminated from consideration. There is a myriad of subjects that could conceivably be decided. . . . The subjects that do become part of the decisional agenda, therefore, represent only a part of the population of subjects that are potential agenda items. This selection of which subjects to address and which ones to overlook is a kind of structural "decision" of major consequence. . . . [When] a matter does reach the decisional agenda, the process by which alternatives are evoked and seriously considered is also crucial" (1981, 282–83).

In the judicial realm, for example, judges may dodge contentious cases that might put them at odds with other branches of government by sidestepping constitutional issues. If we were to ignore this, and examine only judicial behavior on the merits in the less contentious cases for which justices resolved the substantive controversy, we might erroneously conclude that there was little or no strategic behavior when in reality it had occurred at the agenda-setting stage.

Thus, in this stage, attention is directed to the factors that explain why a case in which the court resolved the challenge to a statute is on the docket of some state supreme courts but not others. Stated simply, the dependent variable is a docketed judicial review case (DJRC) for which the court granted full hearing on the merits of the controversy regarding the constitutional challenge to a state statute or statutory provision. Recall from earlier discussions, justices can choose not to decide the constitutional fate of state laws. Hence, while litigants must first bring the case to court, justices can and do ultimately dismiss constitutional challenges to state law.[8]

The first consideration is whether judges behave strategically vis-à-vis the preferences of state government. If judges behave strategically they should guide their decisions according to the anticipated reaction from other branches of government. Here strategic behavior would be indicated by an inverse relationship with ideological distance and likelihood of resolving constitutional cases. However, if ideological distance does *not* create a fear of policy retaliation, judges should behave sincerely. Accordingly, when the preferences of the judge are distant from the preferences of state government, judges will be more likely to engage in judicial review, *ceteris paribus*. In other words, there will be fewer cases where judges resolved constitutional challenges to state laws if justices behave sincerely.

Thus,

> H1$_A$: The likelihood of a docketed judicial review case (DJRC) will be lower as ideological distance increases.

Drawing from the separation-of-powers argument, divided government gives a judge more flexibility because in these instances policy retaliation should be more difficult; divided government expands the safety zone and reduces constraint. Drawing from the literature reviewed earlier, judges also should be less fearful of reprisal under divided government than under unified government because statutory or constitutional override of a judge's vote should be less difficult in the former.

It also might be that litigants are more likely to turn to the courts during times of divided government because presumably attempts to repeal a state law were unsuccessful with the other governmental branches. Thus,

> H2$_A$: The likelihood of a DJRC will be higher in states where there is divided government

When rules governing policy retaliation afford more protection to judges, the concerns about retaliation by other actors should be weakened. As a result, one would not expect to see judicial behavior constrained when conditions in the external environment increase the difficulty of policy retaliation. Under some settings, the cost of retaliation is even greater and judges should be less responsive to the other branches of government. As a result, they should be more likely to engage in judicial review. It is easy to see how this logic extends to the difficulty in the amendment procedure as well. Fear of being overturned is a threat that looms over state supreme court justices and is expected to alter their behavior. It is therefore reasonable that a justice will be less concerned about retaliation when the government faces additional costs (or difficulties) for such retaliation. Thus,

> H3$_A$: The likelihood of a DJRC will be higher in states where it is difficult to amend the state constitution.

Research by Hall (1987, 1992, 1995) demonstrates that elected justices perceive their decisions at risk and thus, if elected, justices are likely to alter their behavior when deciding controversial cases. We can extend this logic to the agenda-setting stage of judicial review and expect that the desire for reelection should provide an incentive for justices in legislative and/or gubernatorial retention systems to be more responsive to state government. When not retained by the other branches of government, judges should be particularly less fearful of retaliation from the legislature and governor. Thus,

H4$_A$: The likelihood of a DJRC will be higher in states where justices are not retained by the legislature or governor.

Research by Brace and Hall (1995) and Hall (1992) has demonstrated that the strategic behavior of state supreme court justices varies negatively with term length in death penalty cases. Brace, Hall, and Langer (1999) also find that term length increases the likelihood of judicial review. Justices with longer terms should be less fearful of an adverse retention vote. Extending this logic further, it is expected that justices will be more likely to challenge the preferences of government when they enjoy longer terms. The crux of the argument is that longer terms might provide more time for wounds to heal, particularly in the iterative game of judicial review. Thus,

H5$_A$: The likelihood of a DJRC will be higher as term length increases.

I consider two additional factors that are peripherally related to strategic behavior and directly related to the selection process. The presence of an intermediate appellate court is reasoned to offer additional discretion over dockets (Glick 1991; Tarr and Porter 1988; Brace, Hall, and Langer 1999). State supreme court justices might choose to resolve important constitutional cases because they have more time do so. States with intermediate appellate courts also give litigants another opportunity to raise a constitutional challenge before raising the challenge before the state's court of last resort. As a result, justices might be less likely to dismiss such challenges. Finally, the presence of an intermediate appellate court increases intercourt conflict, which research has demonstrated to be significantly related to the likelihood of judges hearing a case (see, e.g., Ulmer 1983, 1984; Baum 1979). Thus,

H6$_A$: The likelihood of a DJRC will be higher in states that have an intermediate appellate court.

Drawing from the legal model discussed earlier, rights guaranteed by state constitutions—such as the right to vote, right to free speech, right to privacy, and equal protection—are expected to influence the likelihood of judicial review. In these states, we might expect to see a greater number of constitutional challenges to statutes because judges can use the state constitution to afford rights beyond those granted by the United States Supreme Court. Moreover, litigants might feel their chances of winning are better in states where citizens have these fundamental rights guaranteed by their state constitution. Thus,

H7$_A$: The likelihood of a DJRC will be higher in states with constitutional provisions for equal protection, freedom of speech, right to privacy, or right to vote.

EXPECTATIONS ABOUT STAGE II: THE DECISION-ON-THE-MERITS STAGE

Attention in this stage centers on how judges vote in docketed cases. In this stage, hypotheses about strategic and sincere behavior can be tested more directly by considering the ideological nature of the statute in question. Factors are examined that are expected to influence the likelihood of a justice voting to overturn a conservative policy (VOCP) and the likelihood of a justice voting to overturn a liberal policy (VOLP). Also evaluated is the influence of agenda-setting on the decision-on-the-merits. Here, many of the hypotheses tested in the agenda-setting stage are revisited. As before, the models are the same across each area of law, with the exception of controls for case facts and unit or time effects associated with judge, state, and/or year.

A test of whether justices vote strategically should consider the preferences of the justice and ideological nature of the statute. According to the attitudinal model, a judge will be more likely to overturn a statute that is distant from his/her preferences. Thus,

H1$_M$: The likelihood of a VOCP (VOLP) will increase (decrease) with liberal (conservative) justices.

As before, ideological distance between justices and other branches of government is viewed as a threatening situation. Presumably, a state government with liberal leanings will not want a judge to invalidate a liberal statute. Conversely conservative state governments will want judges to invalidate liberal statutes. Thus, as the preferences of state government become more conservative relative to each judge's preferences, judges should be less likely to overturn conservative statutes. Stated differently, if judges are constrained by the preferences of other actors, they will uphold a statute that is consonant ideologically with the preferences of those other actors.[9] Given the measurement of ideological distance, the direction of behavior should be the same. Thus,

> $H2_M$: The likelihood of a VOCP or VOLP varies inversely with ideological distance between the preferences of state government and the justice.

As expected in the agenda-setting stage, justices will be less likely to behave strategically in situations that reduce policy threats (i.e., divided government and difficulty in amendment procedure). Similarly justices are expected to alter their voting behavior in response to situations that enhance or reduce electoral vulnerability (i.e., method of retention and term length). Thus,

> $H3_M$: The likelihood of a VOCP/VOLP will be higher in states where there is divided government.

> $H4_M$: The likelihood of a VOCP/VOLP will be higher in states where it is difficult to amend the state constitution.

> $H5_M$: The likelihood of a VOCP/VOLP will be higher in states where justices are not retained by the legislature or governor.

> $H6_M$: The likelihood of a VOCP/VOLP will be higher in states where justices enjoy longer terms.

Given that the focus is on challenges to the constitutionality of state statutes, it also is important to consider the standard by which courts review these cases.[10] Three standards for reviewing challenges to equal protection or due process are examined: (1) strict scrutiny, (2) intermediate scrutiny, and (3) rational basis. Essentially, under strict scrutiny the court determines whether the legislature had a compelling state interest, which justifies the claimed violation. Similarly, intermediate scrutiny requires the court to consider whether the enacting legislature was protecting a substantial state interest. Strict and intermediate scrutiny often requires that the legislature employ the least intrusive means to protect the state's interest.

Under rational basis (or rationality test), for example, the court must determine whether the enacting legislature had a legitimate state interest to protect and whether this interest reasonably justifies the creation of categories or economic classes. Presumably when the court uses a rational basis test, the likelihood of overturning a statute is much lower than when the court employs a higher standard such as strict or intermediate scrutiny, at least at the federal level. Justice Thurgood Marshall once observed that when legislation is "measured by the mere rationality test . . . that test leaves little doubt about the outcome; the challenged legislation is always upheld" (quoted in Ducat 1978, 223). Thus,

> $H7_M$: The likelihood of a VOCP or VOLP will be higher when the standard of review is strict or intermediate scrutiny.

Two final variables are considered in each of the four areas of law. First, the influence of lower court rulings on the likelihood of voting to overturn a statute is considered. Research demonstrates that judges are significantly more likely to invalidate laws if the lower court found the law unconstitutional (Emmert 1992).[11] Thus,

> $H7_M$: The likelihood of a VOCP or VOLP will be higher if the lower court invalidated the statute.

Finally, existing research has found that when state supreme court justices decide cases on independent state grounds they are more likely to overturn the statute (Friedelbaum 1982; Emmert 1992; Fino 1987). In these instances, intervention by a higher court is limited because raising a federal issue on appeal is difficult. Thus, a decision that rests on independent state grounds reduces the fear of being overturned by other actors, namely, the United States Supreme Court. Thus,

> $H8_M$: The likelihood of a VOCP or VOLP will be higher when justices invoke independent state grounds.

Examination of these hypotheses in both stages of judicial review should provide a better understanding of the separation-of-power forces that shape judicial review. Why judicial review is expected to vary across policy areas and the research design, data, and methodology, are the foci of the next chapter.

Chapter Four

Policy Saliency and Generalizing Behavior in
Judicial Review Cases across Different Policy Areas

Why might some areas of law encourage more strategic behavior than other
areas of law? Why are some policy areas more susceptible to politicization and
consequently more salient to the elected elite? Drawing from Robert Dahl
(1957), Theodore J. Lowi (1964), E. E. Schattschneider (1960), and more
recent work by Frank R. Baumgartner and Bryan D. Jones (1993), the sec-
tions that follow provide some answers to these questions. The scope of
conflict and the type of conflict determine the extent of political repercussions
a policy area might have on state governmental actors, namely, the legislature
and governor. As political repercussions increase, the salience of the policy
area to the elected elite increases. Using this conceptualization, I propose a
framework that places policies along a continuum ranging from most to least
salient to the elected elite.

Dahl (1957) was first to introduce the idea that the likelihood of reviewing and invalidating statutes might vary across different issues. He argued
that countermajoritarian behavior was less prevalent when the issue before
the Court was important to Congress. Fundamentally, issues near and dear to
the legislature seemed to diminish the Court's willingness to challenge legislative majorities.

Also instructive is Lowi's (1964) policy typology. The underlying premise
for Lowi's typology is that policies summon different participants into the
policy arena. He describes "three arenas of power" that characterize the relationships formed among the actors in the policymaking arena. More recently,
Baumgartner and Jones (1993) observed that some policy areas are more

independent from broader political forces than others; quite simply, some policy areas are politicized more (1993, 176–179). Thus, the nature of the policy community varies across policy areas (see also Schattschneider 1960).

Similar logic can be applied to the cases resolved by state supreme court justices. Differences in policy areas are attributed to the actors involved (i.e., scope of conflict) and the ideological nature of the policy (i.e., type of conflict). Both scope and type of conflict are fundamentally tied to the degree of political detriment associated with each policy area. Some areas of law are reasoned to have greater political repercussions for the electoral goals of the legislature and governor. For example, in some areas of law, it is a political necessity to keep judges in line with the preferences of the other actors. The repercussions from inaction by other branches of government in these politically detrimental areas of law are reasoned to loom large and thus create strong incentives for these branches to pay close attention to judicial behavior.

In other areas of law, legislatures and governors can afford to ignore policy votes by justices; these areas are not tied as closely to their electoral or policy goals. The degree of potential benefit or loss that legislators and governors associate with different areas of law is a critical indicator of the political repercussions.

The scope of conflict is one dimension of policy saliency. Scope of conflict refers to the players directly and indirectly involved in the dispute (i.e., winners and losers) and the wherewithal of those players. When the policy before the court invites attention from a greater number of participants, the dispute ignites greater intensity among the participants and judges are expected to be much more responsive to their external environment.

Another important component of scope of conflict is the ease or difficulty associated with mobilization of the players involved. Scholars have argued that the content of the issue affects the mobilization of constituencies. The ease or difficulty in mobilization is said to determine whether the issue is salient and to whom (see, e.g., Lowi 1964; Ripley 1983). Stated differently, some policy areas involve members of the mobilized public. Some areas involve the latent, but easily mobilized public. Finally, other policy areas involve members of the latent public who are difficult to mobilize. Consider, for example, that some actors are more capable and willing to effectively organize and exert influence on state government (Olson 1965), thereby posing more serious threats on governmental ambitions. Organizational costs, on the other hand, can thwart mobilization efforts of other actors, making these actors ineffective against the ambitions of governmental actors. Hence, certain areas of law summon players who pose more formidable threats to the legislature and governor. As a result, judges can become legislative or gubernatorial targets.

A second important dimension is the type of conflict, which essentially depicts the ideological nature of the policy area. The ideological nature of the policy area defines the extent of political ramifications on state government. Jack Walker (1977, 426) astutely remarked two decades ago while studying issue formation and agenda-setting in Congress that some issues "blow up like summer thunderstorms and burst upon the country in magnified form. . . ." Quite simply some issues are more politically charged and ideologically contentious than others. Moreover, some areas of law fall more neatly along a liberal-conservative ideological continuum.

Policy areas that are easily placed into one ideological camp or another often involve issues that resonate with the electorate. Here it is easier for voters to penalize elected officials if they shirk from their ideological camp. Politicians can be held accountable when the policy area splits easily into two camps. The idea builds from R. Douglas Arnold (1991) and his idea of "policy traceability." If there are shades of gray, or multiple ideological camps, it is more difficult to assess blame to a particular ideological camp (or party). Thus, policy areas that can be placed more neatly into one camp versus another camp are more salient to elected elite. The presence and risk of political repercussions are much greater because accountability is higher.

Overall, different areas of law are associated with varying degrees of political repercussions. Essentially, some areas of law are likely to be more politically detrimental to legislators and governors than other areas because they can affect directly the pursuit of political ambitions. Other areas of law are of little consequence to the goals pursued by the legislative and executive branches of government. The political dynamics of the cases and the saliency of the policy are assumed to be a general characteristic of each area of law and not of the particular state in which a case is brought or the specific piece of legislation within the area of law. Political repercussions are assessed in relative terms whereby one area of law is compared to the other areas of law across both dimensions of policy saliency (i.e., scope of conflict and type of conflict).

ASSESSING EACH AREA OF LAW WITH RESPECT TO POLICY SALIENCY

The following are the four areas of law examined in this book:

1. Campaign and election legislation (i.e., high and most direct political repercussions to the state legislature and governor).

2. Workers' compensation legislation (i.e., moderate and more direct political repercussions to the state legislature and governor).

3. Unemployment compensation legislation (i.e., relatively low and less direct political repercussions to the state legislature and governor).

4. Welfare legislation (i.e., few and less direct political repercussions to the state legislature and governor).

Campaign and election law involves conflicts over the expansion or restriction of political participation. Federal campaign and election laws exist, but states are given tremendous discretion to oversee and regulate campaigns and elections. The battle for the White House after the 2000 presidential election makes evident the amount of discretion afforded the states; ballots and voting machines varied tremendously across the states and within states.

Mostly, states determine who participates, under what conditions, the timing and conduct of elections, candidate qualifications, and overall campaign and election procedures and rules. The issues raised in these cases are politically divisive and resonate with the electorate, organized interests, and most directly with the elected elite (Mutch 1988). Historically this area of law also has placed Republicans in direct conflict with Democrats in a battle over political participation and political power. These cases pose severe political repercussions for most actors in the policymaking process, but especially for elected members of the three branches of government. The distribution of political authority, typically at the center of these conflicts, further contributes to the importance of these issues and their controversial nature.

In these cases, state supreme courts must balance their preferences against the preferences of the legislature and governor. Judges anticipate anxiety from other elected institutional actors. The potential for retaliation from governmental actors and judicial responsiveness to these other actors is high. We should therefore see strategic behavior operating most in this area of law.

Constitutional challenges to workers' compensation legislation also should induce a lot of strategic behavior. This area of law is thus reasoned to have significant political repercussions for the elected elite; however, the issues in these cases are less salient to the legislature and governor compared to campaign and election law. As a result, justices are expected to be responsive to strategic considerations, but not as much when compared to strategic voting in campaign and election cases.

Workers' compensation is a form of social insurance that provides coverage for workplace injuries and illnesses. Under workers' compensation, eligible workers receive medical care and rehabilitative treatment, as well as cash payments to partially replace lost wages for time spent away from work. In nearly all states, employer participation is mandatory, and as a result, more than 95 percent of the work force is covered by workers' compensation insurance. Benefits are financed almost entirely by employer premiums paid to commercial insurers or through self-insurance. The insurer has primary responsibility for paying injured workers' claims for benefits.

The state provides the regulatory and administrative framework that defines benefit levels, eligibility, and utilization. Thus, workers compensation laws often affect a state's monetary resources. Much of the legislation passed in this area has been in response to constraints on state budgets. To address budget shortfalls, legislatures have reduced benefits, restricted eligibility, and made utilization more cumbersome. Naturally, state supreme courts have become pivotal players in this area of law.

Workers' compensation legislation often involves conflicts among organized interests such as labor, private business, and insurance carriers. These policies are reasoned to be less salient for elected officials compared to campaign and election cases, but is nonetheless a salient concern for many organized interests and political actors. Drawing from Mancur Olson (1965) and his discussion of costs associated with group formation, business especially, and labor will be most likely to effectively mobilize. These participants can make this area of law politically lethal for many politicians.

Consider also that the issues involved in this area of law can be easily split along liberal versus conservative ideological lines. For example, in many states workers' compensation sparks controversies, and creates winners and losers. The ideological camp associated with the winners and losers are identified without difficulty, making it easier for constituents to pass blame or judgment on members of the state legislature and the governor.

Unemployment compensation legislation is the third area of law examined in this book. This policy area invites a variety of actors into the policy arena; however, unemployment compensation legislation does not attract as many formidable players as workers' compensation laws. Constitutional challenges to unemployment compensation legislation should induce some strategic behavior, but not as much as workers' compensation or campaign and election law. Of the three areas of law discussed thus far, unemployment policy is therefore expected to be least salient to the elected elite.

Unemployment compensation provides partial wage replacement for workers who lose their jobs when there is no longer work available for them. The program creates a unique partnership between states and the federal government. Essentially, the federal government provides broad guidelines and certification requirements. The states establish, oversee, and regulate unemployment insurance programs. Specifically, state laws determine eligibility requirements, benefit duration, and amounts. Under certain circumstances, state legislation also can deny benefits to individuals unable or unavailable for work. Similar to worker compensation, unemployment programs directly affect state budgets. The federal government, however, assumes responsibility for a significant portion of the monetary burdens unemployment compensation creates. Also unlike worker compensation programs, unemployment insurance is often viewed as a public assistance program or aid to the needy.

During the recessions in the early 1980s and 1990s, most states reduced unemployed worker benefits and tightened eligibility standards. Most challenges to unemployment compensation legislation involve unemployed workers and state regulatory agencies; however, in many instances labor organizations and businesses become involved. As a result, this area of law has some political repercussions on state officials. Effective mobilization is less likely in this area of law compared to the area of workers' compensation. Moreover, unlike the previous two areas of law, unemployment compensation fits less neatly into an ideological camp.

Constitutional challenges to legislation regulating welfare benefits comprise the cases reasoned to be the least salient area of law of the four examined in this book. This area of law almost always involves conflicts between the state and an indigent person. State welfare programs emerged from the Great Society Acts of the 1960s, which were intended to provide safety nets for the poor and disabled. Similar to unemployment compensation programs, welfare laws also create partnerships between states and the federal government. Many states also have separate welfare systems beyond those that are encouraged (or required) by the federal government. Federal laws set general guidelines and standards, but state legislation dictates most of the administrative and regulatory framework that determines benefit levels, eligibility, and requirements. Here too, budget constraints often lead to reductions in benefits and more stringent eligibility standards and requirements.

The issues raised in welfare cases are ideologically charged, but because welfare covers both indigent persons (e.g., aid to families with dependent children) and disabled persons (e.g., aid to the blind) this issue area often crosses partisan lines. This makes it more difficult for voters to hold politicians accountable for such policies. Moreover, many of the programs for the indigent raise issues that cross partisan lines (e.g., welfare work-for-aid programs).

Most, if not all, of the litigants involved in these cases are least likely to forge a formidable threat to the legislature and governor. Since organized interests representing the "have-nots" confront greater formation costs than organized interests representing business (Olson 1965), cases that involve indigent or disadvantaged persons, for example, can be reasonably categorized as areas of law with fewer political repercussions than campaign and election laws. These cases are thus reasoned to be of a lower level of salience to the three branches of government compared to the other areas of law. As a result, we would not expect to see judicial behavior in this area influenced as much by strategic external stimuli.

Figure 4.1 illustrates the degree of policy saliency associated with each area of law according to the scope of conflict and type of conflict as discussed in the preceding pages. As the saliency of the area of law increases, policy and electoral threats should be enhanced, encouraging strategic behavior.

Highly salient campaign election cases are expected to induce the most strategic behavior. In this policy area, rules and political contexts that contract the safety zone are expected to deter judicial review most. Justices reviewing

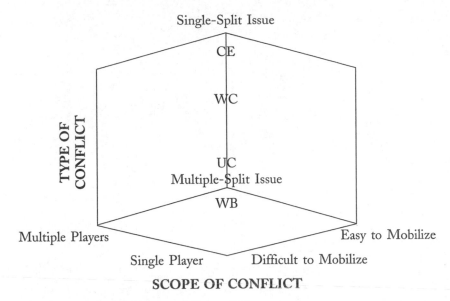

Fig. 4.1. Conceptualization of Policy Saliency

cases involving workers' compensation laws will be less influenced by conditions in their external political environment compared to cases involving campaigns and elections. However, as noted in figure 4.1, these cases are expected nonetheless to encourage strategic behavior. Unemployment compensation cases are expected to encourage the least strategic behavior. Finally, cases involving welfare benefits are expected to encourage sincere behavior because the amount and intensity of interest generated by these cases is quite low relative to campaigns and elections and the costs to the legislature and governor are less severe compared to the other areas of law.

JUDICIAL REVIEW OF CAMPAIGN AND ELECTION LAW

During the 1970 through 1993 period, there were eighty-one judicial review cases in this area of law resolved by state supreme courts in thirty-two states. Figure 4.2 illustrates the types of challenges made to campaign and election laws. Most of the challenges in this area involved campaign disclosure laws (30 percent). These cases were typically disputes about requirements for candidates or elected officials to disclose the amount of campaign contributions to the public. Other cases in this area involved restrictions on placing anonymous campaign ads as well as challenges to laws regulating campaign expenditures

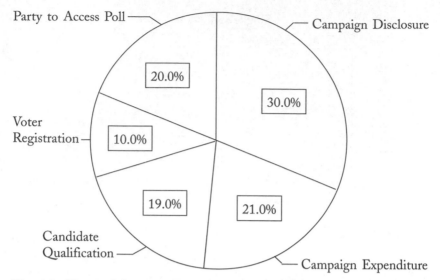

Fig. 4.2. Types of Statutes Challenged in Judicial Review Cases Involving Campaign and Election Laws on State Supreme Court Dockets, 1970–93

NOTE: There were 81 cases involving consitutional challenges to campaign and election legislation during this period.

and donations. As figure 4.2 shows, the amount of money a person or organization could contribute to a candidate or party came under fire in 21 percent of these cases.

The three remaining categories in this area of law pertain to who can participate in the political process. Laws regulating candidate qualifications for office constituted 19 percent of these cases. Here, residency requirements and filing dates were typical of the challenges made. Another type of challenge included laws stipulating voter qualifications (approximately 10 percent of the cases). These cases often involved statutes regulating voter eligibility, such as voter residency requirements. Signature requirements for placing a candidate's name on the ballot and other similar regulations on party access to the polls constituted the remaining 20 percent of the cases in this area of law.

JUDICIAL REVIEW OF WORKERS' COMPENSATION LAW

There were 237 cases in which state supreme courts decided the constitutional fate of workers' compensation laws during the 1970 through 1993 period. Figure 4.3 illustrates the types of challenges that were made in this

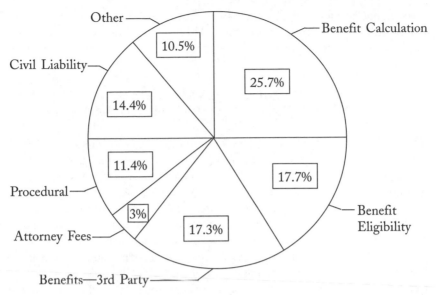

Fig. 4.3. Types of Statutes Challenged in Judicial Review Cases Involving Workers' Compensation Laws on State Supreme Court Dockets, 1970–93

NOTE: There were 237 cases involving constitutional challenges to workers' compensation legislation during this period.

area of law. The largest category involved challenges to legislation regulating the calculation of benefits. Examples of these types of statutes include monetary caps on disability types, classification of injuries, duration of benefits, adjustments for receipt of other income sources, and so forth. Almost 26 percent of the cases involved challenges to these types of statutes, which always reduced the benefit. The next largest category comprised almost 18 percent of the cases and involved challenges to statutes regulating the eligibility for receipt of benefits. In many of these statutes, separate occupational classifications were made to determine who qualified for benefits. Often the challenges to statutes in this category were found in violation of equal protection. These statutes always restricted eligibility.

Statutes prohibiting third parties from collecting workers' compensation comprised 17 percent of these cases. In these cases, the statute in question generally excluded spouses or parents, for example, from collecting workers' compensation if the injured person died. Other issues in this area of law involved challenges to statutes restricting the employees' right to sue the employer for additional costs (i.e., 14 percent of cases). Workers' compensation legislation also involved procedural issues such as filing requirements and certain appellate matters. Finally, a small, but controversial part of the legislation in this area involved attorney fees. With the exception of the latter two categories, the statutes challenged in these cases were conservative in nature.

JUDICIAL REVIEW OF
UNEMPLOYMENT COMPENSATION LAW

There were forty cases during the 1970 through 1993 period in which a constitutional challenge to an unemployment compensation statute was resolved by the state supreme court. As figure 4.4 shows, the statutes challenged in these cases cover an array of issues. Almost 70 percent of these cases involved challenges to conservative statutes. For example, statutes that denied unemployment benefits to women because they terminated employment in order to relocate with their husband were considered conservative. Twenty percent of the cases involved statutes that did not consider domestic or marital reasons good cause for employment termination. Another category reasoned to be ideologically conservative consisted of legislation that denied unemploy-

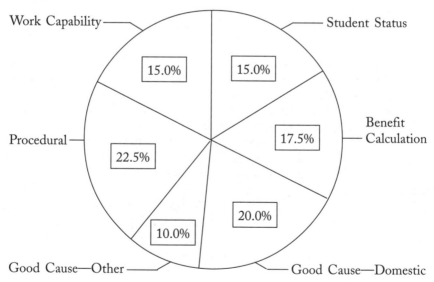

Fig. 4.4. Types of Statutes Challenged in Judicial Review Cases Involving Unemployment Compensation Laws on State Supreme Court Dockets, 1970–93

NOTE: There were 40 cases involving constitutional challenges to unemployment compensation legislation during this period.

ment compensation to persons who were unable to work full time consecutively for thirteen weeks. Work capability statutes constituted 15 percent of
the cases in this area of law. Other examples of statutes in this category
include denial of benefits to the handicapped, the elderly, or to pregnant
women who were unable to maintain consecutive employment for a given
period of time.

Another 15 percent of the cases pertained to statutes that distinguished
between academic status and other forms of employment. The remaining 33
percent of these cases involved legislation that could not be reliably classified
as conservative or liberal. Many of these ambiguous statutes concerned filing
restrictions or other procedural matters (22.5 percent).

JUDICIAL REVIEW OF WELFARE BENEFIT LAW

During the 1970 through 1993 period, state supreme courts decided thirty-
seven constitutional challenges to welfare legislation across sixteen states.
Figure 4.5 illustrates the types of challenges made to welfare laws. State

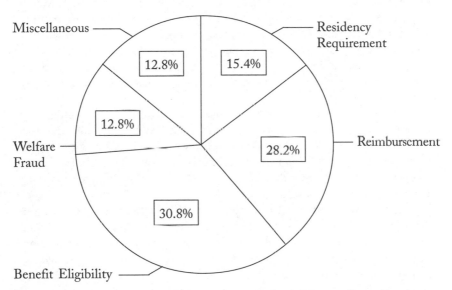

Fig. 4.5. Types of Statutes Challenged in Judicial Review Cases Involving
Welfare Laws on State Supreme Court Dockets, 1970–93

NOTE: There were 37 cases involving constitutional challenges to welfare
legislation during this period.

supreme courts most often decided challenges to statutes restricting benefit eligibility (31 percent of cases). The second largest category involved challenges to statutes that required recipients to reimburse state agencies for the welfare income received. Typically, these cases involved former welfare recipients who inherited a large sum of money. Given the elevated economic status of the former recipient, the state required repayment.

Another proportion of these cases involved challenges to residency stipulations. For example, some states required welfare recipients to legally reside in the state at least one year prior to receiving benefits. For the purposes of this project, challenges to statutes prohibiting certain groups from receiving welfare, limiting the amount of welfare, or restricting the amount of time a recipient can receive welfare are reasoned to be conservative policies. These comprised about 46 percent of the statutes.

RESEARCH DESIGN, DATA, AND METHODOLOGY

Using these data, several hypotheses about sincere and strategic behavior will be evaluated. The research design employed is both comparative and longitudinal across both stages of the judicial process. Existing studies of stage two of judicial review in the states typically employ cross-sectional analysis. Cross-sectional designs are limited because we cannot make inferences about the dynamics of judicial review that change over time. Time series analysis, however, limits our ability to make inferences about the likelihood of reviewing and invalidating statutes across alternative institutional rules and settings.

In the past decades much effort has been devoted to conducting comparative studies of the American states over time and, as a result, the discipline has secured many gains (Brace and Jewett 1995). To continue in that tradition, it is important to examine both stages of judicial review in state supreme courts over a considerable time period. Thus, this study covers twenty-three years across all states.

The literature discussed in chapter two offers a host of reasons why the behavior of judges varies, but perhaps most fundamental are the institutional rules, designs, and political settings within which courts operate. Institutional variation offers a critical advantage to studying state supreme courts. Method of retention of state supreme court justices is one basic component of court autonomy. Table 4.1 illustrates six different methods by which state supreme court justices are retained. These various retention methods afford the actors involved in the process direct opportunities to sanction and reward the members on the bench.

Table 4.1.

Method of Retention for Justices on State Supreme Courts: 1993

Life Tenure or Until Age 70

New Hampshire, Massachusetts, and Rhode Island

---

*Gubernatorial Reappointment or Judicial Nominating Committee
Approved by Governor and/or Legislature*

Delware, Hawaii, Maine, New Jersey,[a] New York

Legislative Reappointment

Connecticut, South Carolina, Vermont, and Virginia

Retention Election

Alaska, Arizona, California, Colorado, Florida, Illinois, Indiana, Iowa, Kansas, Maryland, Missouri, Nebraska, Oklahoma, Pennsylvania, South Dakota, Utah, and Wyoming

---

Popular Election: NonPartisan Elections

Georgia, Idaho, Kentucky, Louisiana, Michigan, Minnesota, Montana, Nevada, New Mexico, North Dakota, Ohio, Oregon, Washington, and Wisconsin

---

Popular Election: Partisan Elections

Alabama, Arkansas, Mississippi, North Carolina, Tennessee, Texas, and West Virginia

---

SOURCE: U.S. Department of Justice, Bureau of Justice Statistics, *State Court Organization*, 1993. Council of State Government *Book of the States*, Lexington: Kentucky.

NOTE: Methods of retention of state supreme court justices have varied across the time period under study.

[a] If reappointed after initial seven-year term, justices serve for life.

Presumably, method of retention shapes the nature and degree of court autonomy. Some states, Massachusetts for example, resemble the United States Supreme Court in that the justices are appointed for life. In other states, such as Connecticut, Delaware, Maine, New York, South Carolina, Vermont, and Virginia, judges are retained by gubernatorial or legislative reappointment. Judges in these latter states are expected to have greater incentives to engage in strategic behavior because they are directly linked to the other branches of government. Stated differently, they are presumed to operate in less autonomous institutions with respect to the other branches of government.

██ Change Decreased Judicial Autonomy
▒▒ Change Increased Judicial Autonomy
◣◣ No Change to Both the Method of Selection and Retention: Legislative Elections
▨▨ No Change to Both the Method of Selection and Retention: Gubernatorial
▭ No Change to Both the Method of Selection and Retention: Partisan or Nonpartisan Elections

Fig. 4.6. State Supreme Court Justices Method of Retention 1970–93

How judges are retained has been the subject of enormous debate and has sparked much reform in this area. As a result, the method of retention has changed considerably over time, with some states adopting a variety of retention methods (Champagne and Haydel 1993). Figure 4.6 illustrates the variation in method of retention overtime by mapping the states that have reformed their method of retention during the 1970 through 1993 period. Eighteen states adopted a different method of retention during this period. Scholars have noted that reform to the selection and retention of states supreme court judges continues (Champagne and Haydel 1993).

Jurisdiction of state supreme courts and the nature of the judicial process also vary across states. Some state judicial systems have intermediate appellate courts while other state judicial systems do not. Thus, the accessibility to the state's highest court and the process along the way is fundamentally different in states like Illinois, where there is an intermediate appellate court, compared to states like Mississippi, where there is not an intermediate appellate court (see Table 4.2). Recall from earlier discussions, both of these states would still provide judges with the discretion to dismiss or resolve a constitutional challenge to state legislation.

Rules defining the process to amend state constitutions also contribute to unique constitutional environments. Recall that difficulty in the procedure to amend state constitutions is expected to inhibit reviewing and invalidating statutes. Table 4.3 identifies the states according to high or low difficulty for

Table 4.2.

States Adopting Intermediate Appellate Courts as of 1993

States that have not Adopted an Intermediate Appellate Court as of 1993

Delaware, Mississippi, Montana, Nevada, New Hampshire, Rhode Island, South Dakota, Vermont, West Virginia, Wyoming

States that have Adopted an Intermediate Appellate Court by 1970

Alabama, Arizona, California, Colorado, Florida, Georgia, Illinois, Indiana, Iowa, Kansas, Kentucky, Louisiana, Maine, Maryland, Massachusetts, Michiga, Missouri, Nebraska, New Jersey, New Mexico, New York, North Carolina, Ohio, Oklahoma, Oregon, Pennsylavania, Tennessee, Texas, Washington, Wisconsin

States that have Adopted an Intermediate Appellate Court in 1979

Arkansas and Hawaii

States that have Adopted an Intermediate Appellate Court between 1980 and 1985

Alaska, Idaho, Connecticut, Minnesota, Virginia

States that have Adopted an Intermediate Appellate Court between 1989 and 1990

Utah and North Dakota

SOURCE: Council of State Government, *Book of the States*, Lexington: Kentucky, various years; U.S. Department of Justice, Bureau of Justice Statistics, *State Court Organization*, 1993.

Table 4.3.

Difficulty in Amendment Procedure in the American States, 1993

States that Require both 2/3 Vote and Approval by Electorate

Alabama, Alaska, California, Colorado, Connecticut, Delaware, Florida, Georgia, Hawaii, Idaho, Illinois, Kansas, Kentucky, Louisiana, Maine, Maryland, Michigan, Mississippi, Montana, Nebraska, New Hampshire, New Jersey, North Carolina, Ohio, South Carolina, Texas, Utah, Washington, West Virginia, Wyoming

States that Require Approval by Two Legislative Sessions

Delaware, Indiana, Iowa, Massachusetts, Nevada, New York, Pennsylvania, South Carolina, Tennessee, Vermont, Virginia, Wisconsin

SOURCE: Council of State Government, *Book of the States*, Lexington: Kentucky, various years.

the legislature to amend the state constitution. In 1993, for example, thirty states required a two-thirds vote in the legislature and approval by the electorate. As a result, modifications to the state constitution are more difficult compared to states not requiring approval by the electorate or a two-thirds vote in the legislature.

Table 4.4.
Average State Supreme Court Ideology by State, 1970–93

State	Mean Ideology	State	Mean Ideology
Hawaii	112.07	New Mexico	41.98
Rhode Island	103.12	Montana	41.58
Maryland	97.39	Utah	41.17
Massachusetts	69.73	Oklahoma CR	41.15
New York	68.30	Wyoming	40.98
Connecticut	67.33	North Dakota	40.84
California	60.04	Florida	40.25
Maine	58.37	Wisconsin	39.06
West Virginia	57.14	Ohio	37.53
Michigan	56.71	Virginia	37.45
Oregon	55.76	South Dakota	34.39
Vermont	55.14	Texas CR	33.94
Pennsylvania	54.24	North Carolina	33.38
Alaska	53.79	Alabama	33.24
Missouri	50.44	Georgia	32.85
Illinois	48.86	Louisiana	32.56
Minnesota	48.34	Texas	32.46
Tennessee	47.35	Nevada	31.99
Kentucky	47.33	Indiana	31.36
Washington	46.94	Idaho	31.23
New Jersey	45.97	Nebraska	29.39
South Carolina	44.76	Kansas	27.07
Delaware	43.41	Iowa	26.25
Oklahoma	43.14	New Hampshire	26.16
Colorado	42.90	Mississippi	25.39
Arkansas	42.86	Arizona	25.03

SOURCE: Data from Paul Brace, Laura Langer, and Melinda Gann Hall, "Measuring the Preferences of State Supreme Court Judges," *Journal of Politics* 62 (2000): 387–413.

NOTE: States are listed in descending order of liberal ideology. CR indicates state supreme court for criminal appeals. For the analyses, measures were rescaled to fit 0 to 100 range.

These institutional rules have changed both across states and overtime permitting comparative inquiry of this important component of American politics. State supreme courts are expected to operate differently under these various institutional settings and comparative inquiry can help disentangle the complexity of forces influencing judicial review at both stages.

The constitutional provisions state supreme court justices apply when settling disputes also vary across the states. Not only does the content of state constitutions differ from the United States Constitution, but also state constitutions tend to be longer and more detailed. Many state constitutions explicitly incorporate an array of citizen rights beyond the rights afforded in the United States Constitution. For example, an increasing number of states have adopted constitutional amendments protecting the right to privacy. Other states have adopted rights to public welfare (e.g., New York). Even more states have adopted equal protection provisions affording greater protection beyond the Equal Protection Clause in the United States Constitution.

Finally, the ideological preferences of judges are critically important features of states. Table 4.4 illustrates state supreme court justice ideology for the 1970 through 1993 period. As the table illustrates, supreme court justice ideology varies widely. Hawaii ranks highest during this period as having the most liberal aggregated preferences, whereas the average of Arizona's justices is the most conservative in the country for this time period.

Clearly, the variation in institutional rules, context, and preferences provides enormous analytical leverage in studying the likelihood of courts reviewing and invalidating statutes. As a result, an examination of state supreme courts and the likelihood of reviewing and invalidating statutes can advance our understanding of sincere and strategic voting and the role of the courts' in the policymaking process. The following section provides a discussion of the data used to examine this phenomenon.

Case Identification and Coding

Cases were collected using Lexis-Nexis and Westlaw in each of the fifty states for the 1970 through 1993 period (see the appendix for the search languages). Given that the central focus in this book is with the responsiveness of state supreme court justices to state legislatures and governors, cases involving challenges to county or municipal ordinances were excluded.[1] Moreover, local governments often operate under different rules and do not have any authoritative checks over state supreme courts.

Combined the searches produced 689 campaign and election cases; 300 workers' compensation cases; 201 welfare and unemployment compensation cases; and 22 cases from the footnotes or citations within these cases.[2] However, to ensure the validity and reliability of these data, ten of the 1,212 cases were given to a professor of public law and a practicing constitutional lawyer.[3] For the purposes of this book, validity was examined with respect to whether or not the court ruled on the issue of constitutionality of the state statute. Also examined was the standard of review invoked by the court to evaluate the constitutional challenge.

The search language was intended to identify only cases in which state supreme courts decided the constitutional fate of state legislation in the four areas of law. Some of the cases identified, however, did not meet these criteria. Thus, each of the 1,212 cases was then read in its entirety by the author to identify those cases where (1) the court ruled on the merits, regarding the challenge to the constitutionality of a state statute, and (2) the subject matter of the challenged statute or provision. As a result, 395 relevant cases were identified and were coded by the author.

The following characteristics were coded for each of these 395 cases:

- whether the court ruled on the issue of constitutionality of the statute
- whether the court invalidated or upheld the statute in question
- year of state supreme court decision
- lower court participation and outcome
- each individual judges' vote to invalidate or uphold the statute in question
- each individual judges' opinion behavior (i.e., dissent, concur)
- each individual judges' outcome vote (e.g., favoring injured worker)
- the substantive issue in the case (i.e., of the statute)
- the date of the statute in question
- the standard of review employed by the court
- the primary constitutional violation
- the party challenging the constitutionality of statute (e.g., injured worker)
- the party supporting the constitutionality of statute (e.g., insurance agency)
- whether amici briefs were filed
- whether the case involved a class-action suit
- the winning party (e.g., injured worker, insurance agency)
- agency involvement and
- original court that heard the case

Inter-coder reliability was then conducted on 378 cases of the 395 for the following variables: (1) whether the court ruled on the issue of constitutionality of the statute; (2) whether the court invalidated or upheld the statute in question; (3) whether the individual judges in each case voted to invalidate or

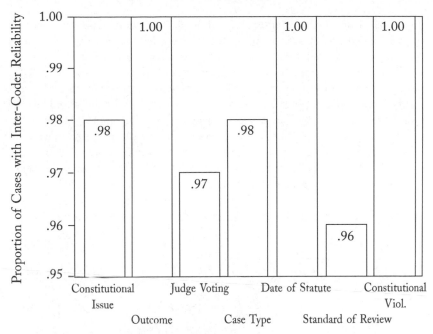

Fig. 4.7. Inter-coder Reliability by Question

NOTE: There were 365 cases in this round of reliability tests. Combined, 95 percent of the cases were included in the inter-coder reliability tests.

uphold the statute in question; (4) the substantive issue in the case; (5) the date of the statute in question; (6) the standard of review employed by the court; and (7) the primary constitutional violation.[4]

Reliability tests were conducted in two increments. The first round consisted of thirty-five cases, after which differences were discussed and the coding scheme and template were revised. The proportion of questions for which we both coded the same was relatively high, but not high enough for statistical standards.[5] In the second round of inter-coder reliability, 343 new cases were coded. The results of these reliability tests are presented in figure 4.7. The lowest inter-coder reliability score is 96 percent for standard of review. Moreover, three of the seven questions coded attained 100 percent inter-coder reliability.

Selection of Cases and Case Characteristics

The theoretical reasons for selecting campaign and election law, workers' compensation law, unemployment compensation law, and welfare law were

discussed earlier in this chapter. The following section discusses the methodological and practical considerations that also guided the selection of cases for
this project. After much consideration, it was clear that to adequately test the
validity of hypotheses about the responsiveness of judges at both stages of the
judicial process, only a select number of different areas of law could be analyzed. Hence, the approach taken was one that examines the population of
judicial review cases in four different areas of law. This approach overcomes
the practical and methodological limitations that would result from examining the population of judicial review cases for all state supreme courts.

Characteristics of these cases were considered from both a methodological and practical perspectives. First, it was necessary to have sufficient variation for statistical analysis across some important dimensions. Cases that are
quite distinct from each other would create difficulties in ascertaining whether

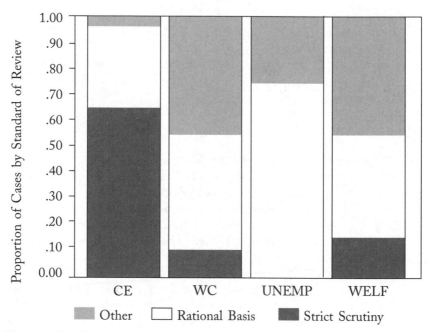

Fig. 4.8. Standard of Review by Area of Law for Judicial Review Cases on
State Supreme Court Dockets, 1970–93

NOTE: There were 81 cases in which a consitutional challenge was made to
state statutes for campaigns and elections (CE); 237 for workers' compensation (WC); 40 for unemployment compensation (UNEMP); and 37 for welfare
(WELF). The category for strict scrutiny also includes intermediate scrutiny.

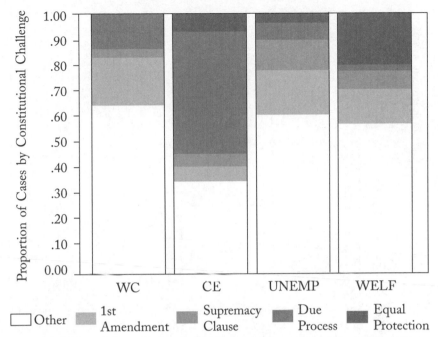

Fig. 4.9. Type of Constitutional Challenge made to statute by Area of Law for Judicial Review Cases on State Supreme Court Dockets, 1970–93

NOTE: There were 81 cases in which a consitutional challenge was made to state statutes for campaigns and elections (CE); 237 for workers' compensation (WC); 40 for unemployment compensation (UNEMP); and 37 for welfare (WELF).

differences in judicial behavior are due to the idiosyncrasies of the cases or the political dynamics expected to vary in these areas of law.

As figure 4.8 illustrates, each of the areas of law has cases in which rational basis or strict scrutiny was employed as the standard of review for the issue of constitutionality. Variation along this dimension permits an examination of the standard of review employed by the courts across each area of law. Specifically, it allows a test of differences between rational basis and strict scrutiny. In these cases, the court utilized a rational basis test in 32 percent of the campaigns and elections judicial review cases, 45 percent in the welfare cases, 46 percent in challenges to workers' compensation laws, and a high of 72.5 percent in cases involving challenges to unemployment compensation laws (see fig. 4.8).

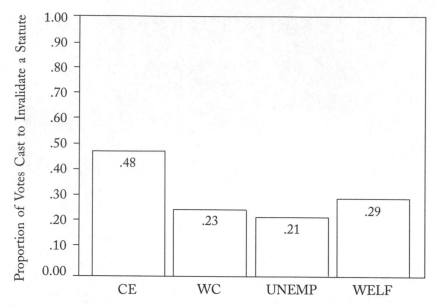

Fig. 4.10. Proportion of Individual Justices' Votes Invalidating the statute challenged, by Area of Law for Judicial Review Cases on State Supreme Court Dockets, 1970–93

NOTE: There were 462 individual votes on the constitutionality of statutes for campaign and elections (CE); 1,478 for workers' compensation (WC); 212 for unemployment compensation (UNEMP); and 163 for welfare (WELF).

Another consideration is the type of constitutional challenge made to the state statute. While the subject matter of the legislation differs, the constitutional violation found in these cases is an important underlying dimension. Figure 4.9 illustrates that these areas of law are primarily about equal protection, due process, and the supremacy clause. With the exception of challenges to campaign and election laws, over 50 percent of the cases involved an equal protection challenge, with campaign and elections comprising 40 percent.

Finally, it is important to consider the variation in the individual votes to invalidate (or uphold) the statute in question. Figure 4.10 provides the proportions of individual judges casting a vote to invalidate a statute across each area of law. Almost 50 percent of the votes cast in cases challenging campaign and election legislation were votes to invalidate the statute. The frequency of justices casting a vote to invalidate a welfare law also was relatively high at 30 percent. In the unemployment cases, state supreme court justices voted to invalidate the statute only 21 percent of the time. Justices also seemed hesitant to vote to invalidate workers' compensation statutes (23 percent).

Another consideration is the distribution of the cases across states and over time. If there were a total of thirty-seven cases appearing on state supreme court dockets in 1970 and 1971, it would be difficult to test temporal hypotheses. Moreover, a concentration of cases in only one or two states would limit the degree of generalization this study can make. Examining a time frame spanning twenty-three years provides longitudinal depth to this study. The time frame also corresponds well with the availability of data on the biographical characteristics of judges that was necessary to estimate judge ideology, ideological distance, and identify natural courts.

Tables 4.5, 4.6, 4.7, and 4.8 list the states and years in which the cases in these areas of law were on the dockets of state supreme courts. As the tables illustrate, state supreme courts resolved constitutional challenges to campaign and election laws in thirty-two states in twenty-two different years. There were fewer challenges to unemployment and welfare legislation resolved by state supreme courts (nineteen and sixteen states, respectively). Conversely, almost every state supreme court during the 1970 through 1993 period decided the constitutional fate of workers' compensation statutes.

Table 4.5.
Campaigns and Elections Case Citations

State	Year	Case Citation
Alabama*	1981	403 So.2d 197
Alaska	1974	526 P.2d 1131
Alaska	1977	559 P.2d 80
Alaska	1980	626 P.2d 81
Alaska	1982	651 P.2d 1
Alaska	1983	660 P.2d 1192
Arkansas	1993	858 S.W.2D 684
California	1970	466 P.2d 85
California	1971	487 P.2d 1224
California	1974	521 P.2D 113
California	1976	547 P.2D 1386
California	1979	599 P.2D 46
California	1991	816 P.2D 1300
California	1992	822 P.2d 875
Colorado`	1998	752 P.2D 80
Colorado	1991	817 P.2D 998
Connecticut	1978	402 A.2D 763
Connecticut	1987	526 A.2D 1297
Delaware*	1972	295 A.2d 718
Florida	1971	245 So.2d 53

(continued)

Table 4.5. *(continued)*
Campaigns and Elections Case Citations

State	Year	Case Citation
Florida	1972	259 So.2d 146
Florida	1977	345 So. 2d 330
Florida	1979	372 So. 2d 427
Florida	1981	408 So.2d 211
Florida	1982	425 So. 2d 1126
Florida	1990	561 So. 2d 263
Florida`	1992	604 So. 2D 477
Georgia	1974	208 S. E. 2d 68
Georgia	1977	236 S. E. 2D 617
Georgia	1993	426 S. E. 2D 890
Hawaii	1984	688 P.2d 1152
Illinois	1972	289 N. E. 2D 409
Illinois	1987	506 N. E. 2D 1284
Iowa	1983	331 N. W. 2d 862
Kansas	1980	620 p. 2d 834
Kentucky	1976	540 S. W. 2d 873
Kentucky	1990	798 S. W. 2d 947
Louisiana	1975	328 So. 2d 110
Louisiana	1976	335 So. 2d 438
Louisiana	1982	416 So. 2d 928
Louisiana	1989	545 So. 2d 1031
Louisiana	1990	566 So. 2d 623
Maine*	1983	461 A. 2d 701
Massachusetts	1975	329 N. E. 2d 706
Michigan*	1976	242 N. W. 2d 396
Michigan	1982	317 N. W. 2D 1
Minnesota	1976	244 N. W. 2D 672
Minnesota	1979	284 N. W. 2d 174
Missouri	1972	483 S. W. 2D 70
Missouri	1977	561 S. W. 2D 339
Missouri	1984	669 S. W. 2D 215
Montana	1981	632 P. 2D 300
Nebraska	1983	330 N. W. 2D 136
Nevada	1976	549 P. 2D 332
New Hampshire*	1974	330 A. 2d 774 114
New Hampshire*	1981	430 A.2d 1137
New Jersey	1978	405 A.2D 350
New Jersey	1980	411 A.2D 168
New Mexico	1974	529 P.2D 745
New York	1975	329 N. E. 2d 176
North Carolina	1993	432 S. E. D 832
North Dakota	1978	262 N. W. 2D 731

(continued)

Table 4.5. *(continued)*
Campaigns and Elections Case Citations

State	Year	Case Citation
North Dakota	1981	306 N. W. 2D 614
Oklahoma	1976	554 P. 2D 774
Oregon	1975	535 P. 2D 541
Oregon	1988	750 P.2D 1147
Oregon	1989	783 P.2D 7
Pennsylvania	1980	422 A.2D 124
Tennessee	1977	555 S. W. 2D 1–2
Tennessee	1979	577 S. W. 2D 190
Tennessee	1982	633 S. W. 2d 306
Tennessee	1987	731 S. W. 2D 897
Tennessee	1990	802 S. W. 2d 210
Texas	1979	583 S. W. 2D 338
Washington	1973	512 P. 2D 721
Washington	1974	517 P.2D 911
Washington	1977	569 P.2d 1135
West Virginia	1976	223 S. E. 2D 607
West Virginia	1980	270 S. E. 2D 654
Wisconsin	1979	287 N. W. 2D 519
Wisconsin	1990	456 N. W. 2D 809

*Cases included in stage one but not included in stage two.

Table 4.6.
Workers' Compensation Case Citations

State	Year	Citation
Arizona	1971	490 P. 828
Connecticut	1971	285 A. 2d 318
Illinois	1971	271 N. E. 2d 884
Louisiana	1971	256 So. 2d 122
Mississippi	1971	246 So. 2d 92
Ohio	1971	267 N. E. 2d 318
Oregon	1971	485 P. 2d 1195
Pennsylvania	1971	275 A. 2d 58
Tennessee	1971	469 S. W. 2d 135
West Virginia	1971	184 S. E. 2d 127
California	1972	493 P. 2d 1165
Colorado	1972	493 P. 2d 344
Florida	1972	268 So. 2d 363
Michigan	1972	202 N. W. 2d 786
Minnesota	1972	197 N. W. 2d 443
Nebraska	1972	503 P. 2d 52

(continued)

Table 4.6. *(continued)*
Workers' Compensation Case Citations

State	Year	Citation
Ohio	1972	290 N. E. 2d 181
Rhode Island	1972	294 A. 2d 398
Tennessee	1972	479 S. W. 2d 806
Colorado	1973	512 P. 2d 625
Idaho	1973	511 P. 2d 282
Minnesota	1973	205 N. W. 2d 318
Nebraska	1973	212 N. W. 2d 704
New Hampshire	1973	300 A. 2d 732
Texas	1973	479 S. W. 2d 283
Washington	1973	510 P. 2d 818
Kentucky	1974	508 S. W. 2d 785
Minnesota	1974	215 N. W. 2d 615
Oklahoma	1974	526 P. 2d 1150
Wyoming	1974	521 P. 2d 571
Alaska	1975	544 P. 2d 82
Arkansas	1975	528 S. W. 2d 646
Florida	1975	310 So. 2d 4
Kentucky	1975	519 S. W. 2d 390
Maryland	1975	334 A. 2d 89
Montana	1975	533 P. 2d 1095
Montana	1975	531 P. 2d 1335
Ohio	1975	322 N. E. 2d 880
Oklahoma	1975	534 P. 2d 1282
West Virginia	1975	219 S. E. 2d 361
Arizona	1976	547 P. 2d 473
Colorado	1976	550 P. 2d 856
Colorado	1976	549 P. 2d 780
Colorado	1976	548 P. 2d 914
Colorado	1976	545 P. 2d 712
Connecticut	1976	370 A. 2d 1061
Maryland	1976	366 A. 2d 55
Michigan	1976	247 N. W. 2d 764
Oklahoma	1976	550 P. 2d 1330
Utah	1976	555 P. 2d 293
Washington	1976	550 P. 2d 522
Alabama	1977	344 So. 2d 1216
Arkansas	1977	545 S. W. 2d 604
Colorado	1977	572 P. 2D 836
Georgia	1977	236 S. E. 2d 583
Kansas	1977	563 P. 2d 431
Kentucky	1977	549 S. W. 2d 91
Maryland	1977	369 A. 2d 82

(continued)

Table 4.6. *(continued)*
Workers' Compensation Case Citations

State	Year	Citation
Michigan	1977	258 N. W. 2d 414
Michigan	1977	253 N. W. 2d 114
New Jersey	1977	379 A. 2d 848
Utah	1977	561 P. 2d 690
Wyoming	1977	569 P. 2d 95
Alabama	1978	358 So. 2d 1015
Alabama	1978	359 So. 2d 785
California	1978	583 P. 2d 151
Colorado	1978	581 P. 2d 734
Colorado	1978	580 P. 2d 794
Florida	1978	359 So. 2d 427
Georgia	1978	247 S. e. 2d 874
Maryland	1978	384 A. 2d 748
Nevada	1978	581 P. 2d 859
Nevada	1978	578 P. 2d 752
Utah	1978	576 P. 2d 1297
West Virginia	1978	244 S. e. 2d 327
West Virginia	1978	242 S. E. 2d 443
Alabama	1979	370 So. 2d 947
Alaska	1979	605 P. 2d 426
Indiana	1979	388 N. E. 2d 536
Minnesota	1979	283 N. W. 2d 909
Missouri	1979	588 S. w. 2d 489
Missouri	1979	583 S. W. 2d 162
Montana	1979	587 P. 2d 933
Wyoming	1979	593 P. 2d 182
Alabama	1980	394 So. 2d 1
Arizona	1980	619 P. 2d 736
Florida	1980	389 So. 2d 639
Florida	1980	384 So. 2d 650
Florida	1980	381 So. 2d 1356
Georgia	1980	271 S. E. 2d 178
Minnesota	1980	289 N. W. 2d 486
Montana	1980	606 P. 2d 507
Ohio	1980	416 N. E. 2d 601
Ohio	1980	413 N. E. 2d 809
Oklahoma	1980	621 P. 2d 1148
Pennsylvania	1980	412 A. 2d 1094
Tennessee	1980	603 S. W. 2d 718
West Virginia	1980	271 S. e. 2d 604
Wisconsin	1980	290 N. W. 2d 276
California	1981	636 P. 2d 1139

(continued)

Table 4.6. *(continued)*
Workers' Compensation Case Citations

State	Year	Citation
Florida	1981	394 So. 2d 994
Idaho	1981	635 P. 2d 962
Illinois	1981	426 N. E. 2d 822
Iowa	1981	308 N. W. 2d 50
Louisiana	1981	397 So. 2d 475
Minnesota	1981	313 N. W. 2d 580
Minnesota	1981	305 N. W. 2d 317
Nebraska	1981	306 N. W. 2d 587
New Hampshire	1981	436 A. 2d 1136
Ohio	1981	424 N. E. 2d 282
Virginia	1981	281 S. E. 2d 897
Wisconsin	1981	302 N. W. 2d 487
Arkansas	1982	627 S. W. 2d 557
Colorado	1982	648 P. 2d 645
Colorado	1982	645 P. 2d 1300
Connecticut	1982	444 A. 2d 225
Indiana	1982	441 N. E. 2d 8
Maine	1982	448 A. 2d 329
Michigan	1982	323 N. W. 2d 912
Michigan	1982	316 N. W. 2d 712
Missouri	1982	640 S. W. 2d 121
Missouri	1982	630 S. W. 2d 82
New Hampshire	1982	446 A. 2d 1174
New Mexico	1982	652 P. 2d 1210
New York	1982	442 N. E. 2d 1191
Ohio	1982	438 N. E. 2d 1167
Ohio	1982	436 N. E. 2d 533
Oklahoma	1982	652 P. 2d 285
Oregon	1982	653 P. 2d 970
Tennessee	1982	639 S. W. 2d 437
Wyoming	1982	641 P. 2d 1247
Alabama	1983	435 So. 2d 1271
Florida	1983	440 So. 2d 1285
Florida	1983	440 So. 2d 1282
Kansas	1983	661 P. 2d 1251
Massachusetts	1983	449 N. E. 2d 641
Minnesota	1983	34 N. W. 2d 285
Ohio	1983	443 N. E. 2d 962
Oklahoma	1983	665 P. 2d 12183
Pennsylvania	1983	469 A. 2d 158
Washington	1983	668 P. 2d 1278
Alaska	1984	687 P. 2d 264

(continued)

Table 4.6. *(continued)*
Workers' Compensation Case Citations

State	Year	Citation
Florida	1984	452 So. 2d 932
Georgia	1984	317 S. E. 2d 189
Iowa	1984	342 N. W. 2d 484
Maine	1984	481 A. 2d 133
Michigan	1984	362 N. W. 2d 684
Ohio	1984	466 N. E. 2d 557
Ohio	1984	462 N. E. 2d 1215
Washington	1984	686 P. 2d 483
Wyoming	1984	691 P. 2d 981
Alaska	1985	694 P. 2d 1160
Florida	1985	475 So. 2d 230
Georgia	1985	324 S. E. 2d 453
Idaho	1985	697 P. 2d 818
Minnesota	1985	369 N. W. 2d 505
New Hampshire	1985	498 A. 2d 741
New York	1985	476 N. E. 2d 304
Virginia	1985	327 S. E. 2d 102
Arizona	1986	716 P. 2d 18
Georgia	1986	343 S. E. 2d 688
Kentucky	1986	705 S. W. 2d 459
Louisiana	1986	490 So. 2d 1386
Mississippi	1986	487 So. 2d 1329
Mississippi	1986	483 So. 2d 1339
New Mexico	1986	726 P. 2d 1381
Utah	1986	720 P. 2d 416
Wyoming	1986	722 P. 2d 151
Arizona	1987	733 P. 2d 290
Louisiana	1987	500 So. 2d 771
Minnesota	1987	415 N. W. 2d 318
Minnesota	1987	402 N. W. 2d 520
Mississippi	1987	511 So. 2d 141
Mississippi	1987	505 So. 2d 1026
Montana	1987	744 P. 2d 895
New Hampshire	1987	534 A. 2d 714
Ohio	1987	505 N. E. 2d 962
Washington	1987	734 P. 2d 478
Wisconsin	1987	401 N. W. 2d 568
Alabama	1988	526 So. 2d 581
Alabama	1988	527 So. 2d 581
Colorado	1988	749 P. 2d 423
Connecticut	1988	546 A. 2d 846
Idaho	1988	760 P. 2d 1171

(continued)

Table 4.6. *(continued)*
Workers' Compensation Case Citations

State	Year	Citation
Michigan	1988	433 N. W. 2d 768
Minnesota	1988	428 N. W. 2d 72
Minnesota	1988	417 N. W. 2d 633
Nebraska	1988	426 N. W. 2d 261
New Hampshire	1988	549 A. 2d 778
Ohio	1988	533 N. E. 2d 321
Oregon	1988	760 P. 2d 846
Pennsylvania	1988	538 A. 2d 862
Rhode Island	1988	543 A. 2d 662
Vermont	1988	543 A. 2d 703
Colorado	1989	774 P. 2d 873
Connecticut	1989	562 A. 2d 505
Connecticut	1989	558 A. 2d 234
Florida	1989	543 So. 2d 204
Idaho	1989	769 P. 2d 577
Iowa	1989	445 N. W. 2d 776
Maine	1989	567 A. 2d 430
Montana	1989	777 P. 2d 862
Nebraska	1989	436 N. W. 2d 533
Ohio	1989	543 N. E. 2d 1169
Vermont	1989	561 A. 2d 415
Alabama	1990	570 So. 2d 648
Alabama	1990	565 So. 2d 633
Hawaii	1990	791 P. 2d 1257
Louisiana	1990	567 So. 2d 75
Michigan	1990	462 N. W. 2d 555
Montana	1990	793 P. 2d 769
Utah	1990	793 P. 2d 362
West Virginia	1990	391 S. E. 2d 350
Wyoming	1990	795 P. 2d 760
Alaska	1991	581 So. 2d 846
Colorado	1991	804 P. 2d 161
Florida	1991	582 So. 2d 1167
Georgia	1991	403 S. E. 2d 41
Georgia	1991	401 S. E. 2d 5
Iowa	1991	476 N. W. 2d 58
Ohio	1991	576 N. E. 2d 722
Washington	1991	822 P. 2d 162
Washington	1991	804 P. 2d 621
Wyoming	1991	811 P. 2d 1
Alaska	1992	823 P. 2d 1241
Kansas	1992	830 P. 2d 41

(continued)

Table 4.6. *(continued)*
Workers' Compensation Case Citations

State	Year	Citation
Minnesota	1992	481 N. W. 2d 47
Montana	1992	827 P. 2d 1279
New Hampshire	1992	609 A. 2d 1216
Wyoming	1992	837 P. 2d 48
Florida	1993	630 So. 2d 537
Georgia	1993	429 S. E. 2d 671
Kansas	1993	853 P. 2d 669
Kentucky	1993	851 S. W. 2d
Massachusetts	1993	612 N. E. 2d 1149
Montana	1993	855 P. 2d 506
Oklahoma	1993	852 P. 2d 150

Table 4.7.
Unemployment Compensation Case Citations

State	Year	Citation
Alaska	1990	790 P. 2d 702
California	1983	663 P. 2d 904
Colorado	1973	515 P. 2d 95
Colorado	1973	508 P. 2d 385
Colorado	1976	556 P. 2d 895
Colorado	1976	550 P. 2d 868
Colorado	1978	576 P. 2d 541
Colorado	1979	593 P. 2d 329
Delaware	1983	460 A. 2d 535
Idaho	1975	540 P. 2d 1341
Idaho	1976	545 P. 2d 473
Idaho	1977	565 P. 2d 1381
Idaho	1978	580 P. 2d 70
Kansas	1974	519 P. 2d 754
Kentucky	1972	482 S. W. 2d 590
Louisiana	1988	531 So. 2d 445
Louisiana	1988	521 So. 2d 406
Louisiana	1989	553 So. 2d 442
Massachusetts	1984	471 N. E. 2d 345
Massachusetts	1986	489 N. E. 2d 994
Michigan	1981	301 N. W. 2d 285
Michigan	1984	363 N. W. 2d 602
Mississippi	1985	463 So. 2d 1076
New Hampshire	1988	547 A. 2d 682
New Mexico	1979	594 P. 2d 1181
New York	1991	585 N. E. 2d 809

(continued)

Table 4.7. *(continued)*
Unemployment Compensation Case Citations

State	Year	Citation
North Dakota	1989	440 N. W. 2d 518
Ohio	1980	414 N. E. 2d 415
Pennsylvania	1983	466 A. 2d 107
South Carolina	1982	298 S. E. 2d 775
South Carolina	1984	316 S. E. 2d 143
Utah	1972	493 P. 2d 614
Utah	1973	509 P. 2d 355
Utah	1975	531 P. 2d 870
Utah	1977	572 P. 2d 1364
Utah	1982	642 P. 2d 719
Utah	1984	678 P. 2d 315
Washington	1972	503 P. 2d 460
Washington	1973	517 P. 2d 599
Washington	1974	525 P. 2d 768
West Virginia	1981	280 S. E. 2d 123

Table 4.8.
Welfare Case Citations

State	Year	Citation
California	1973	516 P. 2d 840
Colorado	1979	599 P. 2d 874
Florida	1980	384 So. 2d 152
Georgia	1980	268 S. E. 2d 906
Idaho	1982	642 P. 2d 553
Illinois	1977	361 N. E. 2d 1118
Kansas	1984	684 P. 2d 379
Massachusetts**	1971	273 N. E. 2d 879
Massachusetts**	1975	333 N. E. 2d 388
Massachusetts	1979	391 N. E. 2d 1217
Minnesota	1986	391 N. W. 2d 767
Minnesota	1993	504 N. W. 2d 198
Missouri	1991	811 S. W. 2d 355
Montana	1971	483 P. 2d 720
Montana	1974	521 P. 2d 1305
Montana	1986	720 P. 2d 1165
Montana	1986	712 P. 2d 1309
Montana	1987	745 P. 2d 1128
New Hampshire	1991	593 A. 2d 238
New Jersey	1979	403 A. 2d 487
New Mexico	1978	582 P. 2d 806

(continued)

Table 4.8. *(continued)*
Welfare Case Citations

State	Year	Citation
New York	1976	356 N. E. 2d 276
New York*	1977	373 N. E. 2d 247
New York	1977	371 N. E. 2d 449
New York	1992	605 N. E. 2d 339
Vermont	1985	496 A. 2d 451
Washington	1976	558 P. 2d 155
Washington	1981	630 P. 2d 925
Washington	1983	657 P. 2d 770
Washington	1986	730 P. 2d 643
Wisconsin	1971	184 N. W. 2d 183
Wisconsin*	1971	191 N. W. 2d 913
Wisconsin	1975	225 N. W. 2d 644
Wisconsin	1992	485 N. W. 2d 21

** Cases included in stage one but not included in stage two.
 * Cases included in stage two but not included in stage one.

Methodology and Selection Process

For the reasons discussed earlier in this chapter, pooled cross-sectional time-series analysis is the appropriate approach to evaluate my hypotheses. While pooled analysis is often more desirable because it combines the strengths of cross-sectional and time-series analysis, pooled designs are not without criticism. With a pooled design the assumptions of constant variance and uncorrelated error terms are often violated (see, e.g., Stimson 1985; Beck and Katz 1995). Thus, in both stages of the analysis, unit effects both across time and over space were tested.

Dependent Variable for Stage I, Agenda-Setting

In this stage, the dependent variable is a dichotomous realization of the continuous probability that the *event* (i.e., a case in which the court resolved a constitutional challenge to a state statute is on the state supreme court's docket) is likely to occur. Thus, the dependent variable is equal to one in the year a state supreme court resolved a constitutional challenge to a state statute pertaining to the area of law being examined, otherwise the variable is zero. Given the nature of these data, event history analysis (EHA) is used to evaluate the impact each independent variable has on the probability of an event occurring or not occurring (see, e.g., Berry and Berry 1990; Allison 1984).[6]

Pooled probit was used to estimate the EHA models. Probit is an appropriate alternative to Ordinary Least Squares (OLS) or linear estimation techniques because of the binary nature of the dependent variable. When the dependent variable is dichotomous, OLS lacks certain desirable statistical properties and thus is inappropriate. For example, OLS can generate certain nonsense predictions, with probability estimates not bound by zero and one. Moreover, the relationship between the independent variables and the dependent variable may be curvilinear. As a result, OLS slope estimates will be biased (Aldrich and Nelson 1984; Liao 1994).

For these reasons, maximum likelihood estimation was used. In these models, the standard z score (or t-statistic) can be computed from the ML estimator and its standard error to assess the statistical significance of each variable. The estimated change in the predicted probability of the factors expected to influence judicial behavior in cases of judicial review also can be easily assessed (Liao 1994; Kaufman 1996).

Dependent Variable for Stage II, Decision-on-the-Merits

In stage two, attention centers on each justice's vote to overturn or uphold a state statute or provision in each area of law. First, the likelihood that a justice will vote to overturn a conservative policy is examined. Second, the likelihood that a justice will vote to overturn a liberal policy is examined when possible. The value of the dependent variable is equal to one if the judge casts a vote to overturn a conservative policy (VOCP), otherwise it is zero. Similarly, the dependent variable is equal to one if the judge votes to overturn a liberal policy (VOLP), zero otherwise. Pooled probit analysis also was used to estimate the models in stage two.

As mentioned earlier, typically scholarly attention focuses on one stage of judicial review or both stages of judicial review treated separately. While theoretical advantages exist for studying both stages of the process, examination of one stage in isolation can have methodological consequences. For example, if a nonrandom selection process in stage one is ignored, coefficient estimates for independent variables in the second stage can be biased and standard errors may be inefficient (Achen 1986; Breen 1996). The presence and severity of these consequences are determined by the degree of correlation between the two stages of judicial review.

An example might help illuminate the selection problem. Consider Christopher H. Achen's discussion of the selection process and determinants of success in graduate school (1986). In his example, scholars wish to know how well grades predict success in graduate school. However, Achen argues that we need to consider the selection process by which students are admitted into the graduate program. One criterion is grades. Since other characteristics also can influence the likelihood of being admitted into graduate school (e.g., letters of recommendation), some students with lower grades are admitted. If these students are also successful, grades will be inversely related to success. We also might find that there is no relationship between grades and success in graduate school. Without controlling for the selection process, results can be misleading. It is easy to envision how such selection. bias could operate on court decisions.

Our understanding of strategic behavior is therefore limited when the nonrandom nature of agenda-setting is omitted from the analysis. Why some states have cases on their dockets and not others describes a selection process expected to be highly political, especially when the resolution of cases determines the fate of state laws. Failure to consider the nonrandom nature of the selection of cases on state supreme court dockets may lead to inaccurate conclusions about strategic behavior.

The two-stage James J. Heckman specification takes into consideration the nonrandom nature of the observed phenomenon in stage one and removes the resulting biases in stage two (Heckman 1979; Achen 1986; Green 1993; Breen 1996). The first step (or stage) in these models is called the "selection model," and step two is referred to as the "outcome model." The Inverse Mill's Ratio (IMR) is estimated from the selection model and is included as one of the independent variables in the outcome model. Heckman models were originally developed to address selection bias in analyses where dependent variables were measured using interval level data. William H. Green (1993) offers a technique that easily extends the Heckman procedure to the estimation of dichotomous dependent variables (see also Breen 1996).[7]

Selection models also were typically derived for estimating two decisions (equations) with the same unit of analysis. For example, if perfect data existed, I would model the decision of each justice to cast a vote on whether or not to hear the case in the selection stage. Using MLE analyses, such a model would provide estimates of the IMR for each individual justice modeled. Next, I would model the outcome stage using each justice's vote to invalidate or uphold the statute in question. The corresponding IMR for each justice estimated in stage one would be included as an independent variable, but only for those judges who voted yes to hear the case.[8] This procedure specifies the nonrandom nature of the selection process.

Unfortunately, individual votes for justices in the selection stage are not available. Instead, I only observe the presence or absence of a docketed judicial review case for each state-year. As a result of the unobserved information, I can only empirically assess whether or not the overall case selection process is random based on the preferences for the median justice on the bench. While the sprit of the technique remains intact, the procedure is amended slightly to account for differences in the unit of analysis and the unobserved phenomenon.

Pooled probit analysis is used to estimate stage one, and the IMR is computed and saved for the next step. To account for the nonrandom nature of agenda setting, I use the preferences of the median justice as the best estimate of every justice on the bench in stage one to produce an IMR for each state-year. Using the preferences of the median justice in stage one understates the impact of the selection process on the second stage. In reality, this is not as good as having an estimate of the IMR for each judge, but it is demonstrated to be better than ignoring the selection process altogether because it removes, at the very least reduces, the biases associated with omitting a variable.

In stage two, I simply duplicate the single IMR that was estimated by state-year for each justice participating in stage two. The information about case selection is thus included in the second stage of the analysis to reduce selection biases. I can then test whether strategic behavior occurs at both stages and whether the two sets of decisions are linked. The results of these analyses are discussed in the next chapter.

Chapter Five

Evidence of Supreme Court Justices' Responsiveness across Four Areas of Law

Results for the models of judicial review developed in the previous chapter are discussed below. In each area of law, findings from both stages of judicial review are presented as well as a brief summary of results. Overall, the models performed reasonably well and my hypotheses about policy saliency and strategic behavior conformed nicely to expectations.

CAMPAIGN AND ELECTION LAW

Results for Stage I: Campaign and Election Law

Table 5.1 presents estimates of the likelihood that a case resolving a challenge to a statute regulating political participation is on the docket. The chi-square (α=.001) indicates that the model is a significantly better fit than the null model. The reduction of error is about 6 percent. With the exception of term length and the hazard probability, all of the variables are statistically significant at the conventional .05 level. Also, most of the variables provide directional support for the hypotheses tested. Overall, the results provide strong evidence that in this area of law, state supreme court dockets are shaped by external stimuli, including the relative preferences of other government actors. Stated differently, state supreme court justices alter their behavior as the institutional rules and strategic conditions in their environment change.

Marginal effects on the probability of a docketed judicial review case (DJRC) challenging campaign and election laws were estimated for the

Table 5.1.

Stage I Probit Analysis of Docketed Judicial Review Cases (DJRC): Constitutional Challenges to Campaign and Election Laws, 1970–93

Variable	Coefficient	s.e.	z	Expectation
Ideological Distance	−.009	.005	−1.96**	$\beta<0$
Divided Government	−.257	.124	−2.07**	$\beta>0$
Amendment Difficulty	.160	.091	1.77*	$\beta>0$
Method of Retention	.407	.200	2.03**	$\beta>0$
Term Length	−.019	.176	−.11	$\beta>0$
Intermediate Appellate Court	.281	.142	1.98**	$\beta>0$
Constitutional Rights	.324	.131	2.46**	$\beta>0$
Electoral Competition	.009	.004	2.17**	$\beta>0$
Hazard Probability	−.011	.008	−1.32*	N. E.
Constant	−2.542	.373	−6.81***	N. E.
Reduction of Error				5.67
Percent Modal Category				93.25
Percent Correctly Predicted				97.15
Chi-square				35.96(11)***
Number of Observations				1200

NOTE: Regressing the estimated residuals against time, state, and region dummy variables tested unit effects. Only the unit effects that were statistically significant were included in the models (i. e., southern states, northeastern states).

N.E. indicates no expectation for this variable and s. e. is the standard error.

***$p \leq .01$, **$p \leq .05$, *$p \leq .10$, one-tailed test.

statistically significant variables in this model, using the sample mean as the baseline probability (.29) and holding all other variables constant (see Table 5.2). When indicated in the text, marginal effects for some variables were also examined using a prior probability of .50 to assess the maximum impact of that variable.

As noted previously, ideological distance between judges and other branches of government is expected to shape behavior. More specifically, ideological distance should increase the likelihood of reviewing statutes if judges are *not* concerned about policy retaliation by these other actors.[1] Thus, when the preferences conflict among the three branches of government, an unconstrained judge would be more likely to review statutes. Presumably if this attitudinal explanation of judicial review were operating in the agenda-setting stage, judges would view these situations (i.e., ideological distance) as opportunities to impose their preferences on issues of public policy. However, this result is contrary to an attitudinal explanation.

Table 5.2.

Marginal Effects for Stage I Probit Analysis: The Likelihood of a DJRC on Campaign & Elections

Variable	All	No Distance	Low Distance	High Distance	No Intermediate Appellate Court	Intermediate Intermediate Appellate Court	Short Term Length	Not retained by Legislature or Governor	Easy to Amend	Difficult to Amend
Ideological Distance	-.0253	—	—	—	-.0161	-.0322	-.0138	-.0276	-.0230	-.0276
Divided Government	-.0293	-.0353	-.0310	-.0229	-.0190	-.0358	-.0150	-.0326	-.0260	-.0322
Amendment Difficulty	.0183	.0220	.0193	.0143	.0119	.0223	.0094	.0203	.0172	.0201
Method of Retention	.0463	.0557	.0490	.0361	.0301	.0565	.0280	—	.0436	.0509
Term Length	N.S.	N.S.	N.S.	N.S.	N.S.	N.S.	N.S.	N.S.	N.S.	N.S.
Intermediate Appellate Court	.0320	.0385	.0338	.0250	—	—	.0164	.0356	.0301	.0351
Constitutional Rights	.0369	.0444	.0390	.0228	.0239	.0450	.0189	.0410	.0347	.0405
Electoral Competition	.0737	.0871	.0804	.0603	.0469	.0871	.0402	.0804	.0670	.0804

NOTE: Marginal effects for each variable are computed when all other variables are at their means or modal categories. Modal categories are as follows: intermediate appellate court, divided government, not retained by legislature or governor, easy-to-amend state constitution, short-term length, and states without certain constitutionally protected rights. Means are as follows: ideological distance, 10.41, and electoral competition, 50.39.

N.S. indicates not statistically significant and thus indistinguishable from zero.

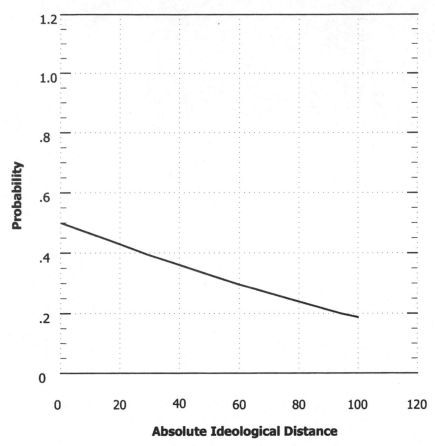

Fig. 5.1. The Effect of Ideological Distance on the Probability of a DJRC on a Campaign and Election Law, Assuming a Prior Probability of .50

Results indicate that fewer statutes are reviewed when the judge's preferences are ideologically distant from the other branches of government (i.e., outside the safety zone). In these instances, an increase in the ideological distance between the judge and the other branches of government is associated with a 2.3 percent decrease in the probability of a DJRC. These campaign and election issues can have important political repercussions on each branch of government, and for these reasons the attitudinal explanation might not be operative in state supreme courts during the agenda-setting stage.

When the preferences of these actors clash, judges react as if they perceive the situation as threatening. Figure 5.1 illustrates the impact of ideological distance on the probability of a DJRC challenging a campaign and election law, assuming a prior probability of .50. As the graph demonstrates, there is a decline in the probability of a DJRC as ideological distance increases. However, when the preferences of the judge and the preferences of the legislature and governor are consonant, judges are indifferent.

Results for political situations expected to reduce fear of policy retaliation also are interesting. The estimated coefficients for divided government and difficulty in amendment procedure depict the degree to which judges react to institutionally induced fears of policy retaliation (Table 5.1). The findings with respect to these two indicators of policy retaliation, however, are mixed. Contrary to expectation, judges operating in a state under divided government are significantly less likely to have a DJRC challenging a campaign and election statute. In these states, the probability of a case being on the state supreme court docket is reduced by 2.9 percent compared to states under unified government. As expected, states where it is more difficult to amend the constitution, judges have a 1.8 percent higher probability of a DJRC challenging campaign and election legislation.

Examination of the marginal effects of amendment procedure across different levels of ideological distance also is informative. Table 5.2 illustrates when the effects of amendment difficulty are attenuated, ideological distance between judges and government grows. Judges are more likely to review legislation in states with difficult constitutional amendment procedure; yet, the probability is reduced as the judge's preferences become more distant relative to the other branches of government.

In terms of electoral threats of retribution, results indicate court dockets are shaped by these fears as well. Length of term is not statistically significant, but method of retention is statistically significant at the .05 level and receives directional support. Judges are almost 5 percent more likely to have a DJRC challenging campaign and election laws when operating in states where they are not retained via the legislature or governor. In these states, fear of electoral retribution imposed by the legislature and governor is removed and justices seem freer to engage in adversarial behavior with these other actors. Stated differently, electoral insularity from other government actors expands the judge's safety zone.

Examination of the marginal impact of retention methods across different levels of ideological distance is also informative. Table 5.2 illustrates that the probability of a DJRC challenging campaign and election laws is 2 percent lower when ideological distance is one standard deviation above average. Thus, the effect of retention method is mitigated when there is greater ideological distance between the judge and the other branches of government. Even when the retention method insulates judges from electoral retribution, judges react as though they fear policy retaliation when there is greater ideological distance. In this area of law, electoral protection afforded by institutional rules does not remove fear of policy retaliation when certain levels of ideological distance are reached.

Finally, the results demonstrate that other institutional and contextual forces shape state supreme court dockets. The presence of an intermediate appellate court significantly increases the probability that the state supreme court will decide constitutional challenges. Here the probability of a DJRC challenging a campaign and election law increases by 3.2 percent in states with intermediate appellate courts. The presence of an intermediate appellate court increases the chances of intercircuit court conflict. As a result, state supreme court judges are often pulled into these disputes as a mediator of lower court disagreement. Such an interpretation comports with a legal-systemic view of agenda-setting, which posits that intercircuit conflict significantly increases the likelihood of getting on the United States Supreme Court's agenda (see, e.g., Ulmer 1983, 1984).

Also as expected, the presence of a constitutionally guarded right to vote, right to privacy, and/or equal protection increases the probability of a DJRC resolving a challenge to a campaign and election law by almost 4 percent compared to states without these rights. These results confirm findings of previous studies of agenda-setting behavior on abortion cases (Brace, Hall, and Langer 1999) and a broader range of campaign and election cases (Langer 1997). Basically, judges in states with stronger constitutional foundations are more likely to intervene.

Given that these cases challenge statutes regulating the distribution of political authority, litigants might expect higher success rates in getting their dispute on the court's docket when the nature of the relationship among the parties is competitive. Interparty competition thus might shape agenda-setting. Comporting with earlier research on state supreme court dockets (Atkins and Glick 1976), the probability of a DJRC challenging a campaign and election law increases by about 7 percent with a one standard deviation increase in interparty electoral competition.

The results discussed above provide compelling evidence that institutional and other contextual variables exert predictable and significant influences on agenda-setting in this area of law. If judges were acting solely on the basis of sincere preferences, or if they were choosing cases strictly on the bases of facts and law, the results presented here would be improbable in the extreme. Clearly, case selection occurs in a nonrandom fashion. This selection process, while interesting in its own right, might also clarify our view of the forces operating in the second stage of judicial review.

Results for Stage II: Campaign and Election Law

Whereas in stage one the concern was with differences between states that did and did not engage in judicial review, attention now turns to 462 individual justices' votes on constitutional challenges to campaign and election laws for 339 different state supreme court justices. Tables 5.3 and 5.4 present the results for stage two. The findings for the likelihood of voting to overturn a conservative policy (VOCP) are presented in Table 5.3. Once again, the overall fit of the model is significantly better than the null model, as indicated by the chi-square (α=.001). The reduction of error in the fitted model is about 3 percent better than the null model. Moreover, only three variables of substantive interest are statistically significant at the .05 level or better. It could be that the selection process, along with the rarity with which justices vote to invalidate conservative statutes in this area of law, are affecting the performance of this model.

If the attitudinal model is operative in this area of law, a justice's sincere preference should significantly influence her vote; ideological distance will not matter. Alternatively, if justices are concerned about the preferences of the legislature and governor, relative preferences of the justices should influence their votes.

A justice's sincere preference might outweigh the effects of ideological distance, providing a simple case of sincere behavior. Alternatively, distance might subordinate the effects of the justice's sincere preferences, providing a clear case of uniformly strategic behavior. There could, however, be another situation where judge ideology and distance operate conditionally. In these instances, sincere preferences are dominant up to some point but beyond that point the effects of distance outweigh sincere preferences, inducing strategic behavior.

In this area of law only ideological distance exerts a statistically significant effect on the probability of a VOCP suggesting that sincere preferences are subordinate to the preferences of the legislature and governor. Figure 5.2 illustrates the effect of ideological distance on the probability of voting to invalidate a conservative campaign and election statute when justice ideology is effectively zero and the prior probability is .50. Since the impact of justice ideology is statistically zero, positive values for ideological distance indicate a move toward more liberal state government and negative values indicate a move in the conservative direction. Thus, beginning at zero and moving along the X-axis from left to right, the probability that a judge will vote to invalidate a conservative campaign and election law increases. When ideological distance is forty, for example, the probability of invalidating a conservative statute jumps to 80 percent from a prior probability of .50. Ideological distance seems to create a politically threatening environment. Justices alter their behavior in response to the preferences of other government actors. This effect of ideological distance is by no means uniform across areas of law.

The results also indicate that other more direct policy and electoral fears of retaliation do not significantly influence a justice's behavior. In these specific types of cases, justices are neither more nor less likely to invalidate statutes

Table 5.3.
Stage II Probit Analysis of Individual Justice's Vote to Overturn Conservative Policy (VOCP) Regarding Campaign and Election Laws, 1970–93

Variable	Model with Selection Process			Model Without Selection Process			Expectation
	coefficient	s.e.	z	coefficient	s.e.	z	
Justice Ideology	-.001	.007	-.14	.001	.007	.08	$\beta>0$
Ideological Distance	.022	.011	1.91**	.018	.011	1.57*	$\beta<0$
Divided Government	.157	.290	.54	.279	.267	1.05	$\beta>0$
Amendment Difficulty	-.181	.323	-.56	-.186	.319	-.58	$\beta>0$
Method of Retention	-.221	.603	-.37	-.553	.511	-1.08	$\beta>0$
Term Length	-.433	.309	-1.40*	-.385	.302	-1.27	$\beta>0$
Independent State Grounds	-.160	.294	-.55	-.330	.259	-1.27	$\beta>0$
Standard of Review	1.420	.465	3.05***	1.447	.468	3.09***	$\beta>0$
Lower Court Invalidates Statute	.258	.433	.60	.198	.432	.46	$\beta>0$
Lower Court Does Not Participate	.875	.344	2.54***	.861	.346	2.49***	N. E.
Residency Requirement	2.290	1.56	1.47*	2.223	.557	3.99***	$\beta>0$
IMR: Selection Variable	.504	.288	1.75**	—		—	N. E.
Constant	-3.737	1.379	-2.71***	-2.649	.943	-2.81**	N. E.
Percent Correctly Predicted	93.69			92.4			
Percent Modal Category	90.90			90.9			
Reduction of Error	2.79			1.5			
Chi-square (degrees of freedom)	54.48 (12)***			53.78 (11)***			
Number of Observations	462			462			

NOTE: Regressing the estimated residuals against time, state, and judge dummy variables tested unit effects. Only the unit effects that were statistically significant were included in the models (i.e., none).

N.E. indicates no expectation for this variable; s. e., is the standard error.

***p $\leq$ .01, **p $\leq$ .05, *p $\leq$ .10, one-tailed test.

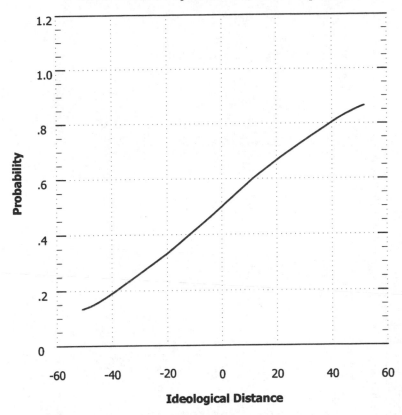

Fig. 5.2. The Effects of Ideological Distance on the Probability of Voting to Invalidate a Conservative Campaign and Election Law, Assuming Judge Ideology has no Impact and a Prior Probability of .50

when political conditions and institutional rules protect them from policy and electoral sanctions. This does not, however, mean that strategic behavior was absent in this area of law. Given that these threats played a significant role in shaping the docket, lack of statistical significance is not too surprising.

Overall, the results in this model provide strong evidence indicating that these justices were influenced by the preferences of state government. Less evidence was found that other external forces shaped votes on the case merits. The operation of these forces at the case selection stage would reduce their impact at the merit stage. Finally, only some elements of a legal model were statistically significant.

Attention turns now to the factors influencing the likelihood of a justice voting to overturn a liberal policy (VOLP). The performance of this model

Table 5.4.

Stage II Probit Analysis of Individual Justice's Vote to Overturn Liberal Policy (VOLP) Regarding Campaign and Election Laws, 1970–93

Variable	Model with Selection Process			Model Without Selection Process			Expectation
	coefficient	s.e.	z	coefficient	s.e.	z	
Justice Ideology	-.004	.002	-1.67**	-.004	.002	-1.72**	$\beta<0$
Ideological Distance	.002	.005	.50	-.003	.005	-.60	$\beta>0$
Divided Government	.408	.195	2.08**	.516	.174	2.95**	$\beta>0$
Amendment Difficulty	.505	.196	2.57***	.606	.186	3.25***	$\beta>0$
Method of Retention	.762	.359	2.11**	.392	.341	1.14	$\beta>0$
Term Length	.445	.177	2.51**	.447	.173	2.58**	$\beta>0$
Independent State Grounds	.148	.193	.76	-.042	.172	-.25	$\beta>0$
Standard of Review	.192	.175	1.09	.050	.174	.28	$\beta>0$
Lower Court Invalidates Statute	1.192	.230	5.17***	.863	.220	3.90***	$\beta>0$
Lower Court Does Not Participate	.187	.200	.94	-.062	.193	-.32	N. E.
Campaign Expenditures	1.74	.206	8.46***	1.71	.199	8.56***	$\beta>0$
IMR: Selection Variable	.869	.280	3.09***	—	—	—	N. E.
Constant	-3.620	.824	-4.40***	-1.64	.426	-3.86***	N. E.
Percent Correctly Predicted	80.50			80.60			
Percent Modal Category	53.20			53.20			
Reduction of Error	27.30			27.41			
Chi-square	170.51 (12)***			159.51 (10)***			
Number of Observations	102			102			

NOTE: Regressing the estimated residuals against time, state, and judge dummy variables tested unit effects. Only the unit effects that were statistically significant were included in the models (i.e., none).

N.E. indicates no expectation for this variable; s.e., is the standard error.

***p ≤ .01, **p ≤ .05, *p ≤ .10, one-tailed test.

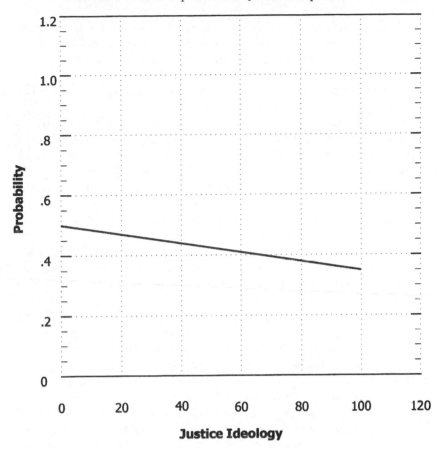

Fig. 5.3. The Effects of Judge Ideology on Probability of Voting to Invalidate a Liberal Campaign and Election Law, Assuming Distance has no Impact and a Prior Probability of .50

is considerably better than the model predicting the vote to overturn conservative policy discussed above. The reduction of error in the fitted model is 27 percent better than the null model and the chi-square is significant at the .001 level (see Table 5.4). In this model, eight of the substantively important variables are statistically significant at the .05 level or better and receive directional support.

Unlike the previous model, justice ideology is statistically significant and inversely related to the likelihood of a VOLP. As expected, liberal justices are less likely to overturn liberal policy. Figure 5.3 illustrates the impact of preferences on the probability of a justice voting to invalidate a liberal statute.

Here a justice with an ideology score of sixty (relatively liberal) is 10 percent less likely to invalidate a liberal policy from a baseline probability of .50. Moreover, a very liberal justice with an ideology score of one hundred has a probability of only .38 of voting to invalidate a liberal policy. Sincere preferences clearly matter. Justices seem to act unconcerned about the preferences of other branches of government.

While appearing less strategic vis-à-vis the preferences of other political actors, rules that heighten fears of policy retaliation seem to shape judicial behavior. Unlike the agenda-setting stage, here divided government significantly increases the likelihood that a justice will vote to invalidate a liberal policy. Similarly, when it is difficult to amend the constitution, justices are significantly more likely to invalidate these types of statutes.

Electoral goals also seemingly shape the votes of justices when deciding whether to invalidate these statutes. As in stage one, justices who are not retained by the legislature or governor are significantly more likely to invalidate statutes. Fear of electoral retribution for these justices is miniscule and, as a result, they appear to be more willing to act according to their own preferences. Also as expected, justices on courts with longer terms are significantly more likely to invalidate liberal statutes. Removed from threats of electoral retribution, justices act as if the legislature and governor have short memories.

Results also indicate that case facts, such as the lower court ruling and the type of campaign and election law, significantly influence the vote on the merits. Unlike the model predicting votes to overturn conservative policy, a lower court's decision to invalidate the statute is positively related to a vote to invalidate a liberal policy.[2] This relationship supports earlier work by Craig F. Emmert (1992), who found a strong relationship between lower court rulings and state supreme court invalidation of statutes. Justices also are significantly more likely to VOLP when the statute regulated campaign expenditures compared to statutes that regulated disclosure of funds. Standard of review in this model was not statistically significant.

The Selection Process for Campaign and Election Law

The models presented above also included another important variable that until now has not been discussed. In both models (i.e., VOCP and VOLP) the selection variable (i.e., IMR) is statistically significant at the .05 level or better. This indicates that the selection process at the docket stage is having a statistically significant impact on votes on the case merits. Tables 5.3 and 5.4 provide the results with and without controlling for the selection process. The overall performances of the models are about the same. However, there are two very important differences in terms of statistical significance. When the selection variable is omitted, ideological distance is not statistically significant at the conventional .05 level for the model explaining the likelihood of a VOCP.

The second important difference is in the model explaining the likelihood of a VOLP. When the selection process is ignored, method of retention is not statistically significant. Thus, in two critical instances, the impact of variables related to strategic behavior are underestimated when the effects of case selection are omitted.

Another way to assess the impact of the agenda-setting stage on the merits stage is to examine the substantive differences in the magnitude of the coefficients across models. For ten of the eleven coefficients estimated, the bias ranged between 2 percent and 250 percent. Variables testing policy retaliation hypotheses are biased most severely. For example, the bias associated with the coefficient for ideological distance ignoring selection was 250 percent. In this instance, the impact was underestimated. Consider also the coefficient on method of retention; ignoring case selection produces an estimate that is biased in the downward direction by almost 50 percent. Clearly an examination of stage two without considering the nonrandom nature of agenda-setting produces biased and inefficient estimators. Inferences about judicial behavior are not as accurate when case selection is ignored.

Summary of Results for Campaign and Election Law

The results from stage one and two offer an important observation: preferences, rules, and political context, significantly influence the likelihood that state supreme judges will review and invalidate campaign and election laws. State supreme court agendas are shaped, in part, by policy and electoral fears of retaliation from the legislature and governor. These same fears influence the votes of justices when they decide whether to invalidate or uphold state law.

WORKERS' COMPENSATION LAW

Results for Stage I: Workers' Compensation Law

Table 5.5 presents the results from the event history analysis on the likelihood of a docketed judicial review case (DJRC) challenging a workers' compensation law. The performance of this model is relatively weak compared to the other models. Only a handful of variables are statistically significant and the reduction of error is less than two percent. The chi-square, however, indicates this model performs better than the null model. Also, most of the variables receive directional support. As before, marginal effects for statistically significant variables were estimated using the sample mean as the baseline probability (.17) with other variables held constant.

Table 5.5.

Stage I Probit Analysis of Docketed Judicial Review Cases (DJRC):
Constitutional Challenges to Workers' Compensation Laws, 1973–93

Variable	Coefficient	s.e.	z	Expectation
Ideological Distance	−.002	.003	−.61	$\beta<0$
Divided Government	.097	.057	1.70**	$\beta>0$
Amendment Difficulty	.145	.093	1.57*	$\beta>0$
Method of Retention	.621	.150	4.14***	$\beta>0$
Term Length	−.065	.137	−.47	$\beta>0$
Intermediate Appellate Court	−.040	.099	−.40	$\beta>0$
Constitutional Rights	.025	.108	.23	$\beta>0$
Income Spent on Workers' Compensation Benefits	.001	.001	1.56*	$\beta>0$
Hazard Probability	.022	.007	3.15***	N. E.
Constant	−44.840	13.740	−3.26***	N. E.
Percent Correctly Predicted				83.25
Percent Modal Category				85.98
Reduction of Error				1.69
Chi-square				35.05(9)***
Number of Observations				1200

NOTE: Regressing the estimated residuals against time, state, and region dummy variables tested unit effects. Only the unit effects that were statistically significant were included in the models (i. e., none).

N.E. indicates no expectation for this variable and s.e., is the standard error.

***$p \leq .01$, **$p \leq .05$, *$p \leq .10$, one-tailed test.

Ideological distance does not significantly influence the agenda-setting stage with respect to workers' compensation cases. State supreme court judges show little concern for legislative and gubernatorial preferences. However, results also indicate that when fear of policy retaliation is presumably weaker, state supreme judges are significantly more likely to resolve a constitutional challenge to a workers' compensation statute. As Table 5.6 illustrates, the probability of a DJRC challenging a workers' compensation statute is 2 percent higher when there is divided government compared to single party control of government. Similarly, the probability of a DJRC challenging a workers' compensation law increases by 3.5 percent in states with difficult amendment procedures compared to states where it is easier to amend the constitution.

These two variables, divided government and amendment difficulty, capture more direct threats of policy retaliation. When it is more difficult for state government to form the coalition necessary to replace a justice's sincere

Table 5.6.

Marginal Effects for Stage I Probit Analysis: The Liklihood of a DJRC on Workers' Compensation

Variable	All	No Distance	Low Distance	High Distance	No Intermediate Appellate Court	Intermediate Appellate Court	Short Term Length	Not Retained by Legislature or Governor	Easy to Amend	Difficult to Amend
Ideological Distance	N.S.	N.S.	N.S.	N.S.	N.S.	N.S.	N.S.	N.S.	N.S.	N.S.
Divided Government	.0201	.0109	.0187	.0176	.0174	.0189	.0099	.0193	.0193	.0215
Amendment Difficulty	.0350	.0362	.0356	.0336	.0332	.0361	.0189	.0383	—	—
Method of Retention	.1499	.1548	.1523	.1435	.1418	.1542	—	—	.0334	.0371
Term Length	N.S.	N.S.	N.S.	N.S.	N.S.	N.S.	N.S.	N.S.	N.S.	N.S.
Intermediate Appellate Court	N.S.	N.S.	N.S.	N.S.	N.S.	N.S.	N.S.	N.S.	N.S.	N.S.
Constitutional Rights	N.S.	N.S.	N.S.	N.S.	N.S.	N.S.	N.S.	N.S.	N.S.	N.S.
Income on Workers' Comp. Benefits	.0245	.0233	.0233	.0212	.0214	.0230	.0490	.0249	.0019	.0019

NOTE: Marginal effects for each variable are computed when all other variables are at their means or modal categories. Modal categories are as follows: intermediate appellate court, divided government, not retained by legislature or governor, easy-to-amend state consitution, short-term length, and states without certain constitutionally protected rights. Means are as follows: ideological distance, 10.41 and workers' compensation (WC) benefits, .206.

N.S. indicates not statistically significant and thus indistinguishable from zero.

preference, judges are much more inclined to engage in contentious behavior. Stated differently, these situations expand the judge's safety zone.

As with challenges to campaign and election law, electoral considerations also influence agenda-setting of workers' compensation cases. The substantive impact of method of retention is very high. Here, the probability of a DJRC challenging a workers' compensation statute is 15 percent higher in states where judges are not subjected to legislative or gubernatorial reappointment. Clearly, when judges do not fear adverse retention votes from the legislature and/or governor, they are more likely to intervene in this area of law.

Other variables expected to shape the selection of cases are not statistically significant. For example, the presence of an intermediate appellate court and constitutionally protected rights did not influence the likelihood of a DJRC challenging a workers' compensation law. Additionally, the amount of money spent on workers' compensation in the state did not significantly improve the fit of the model.

Results for Stage II: Workers' Compensation Law

Attention in this stage centers on 1,478 individual votes on constitutional challenges to workers' compensation laws for 582 different state supreme court justices. Table 5.7 presents the results for the likelihood of a justice casting a vote to overturn a conservative policy (i.e., VOCP).[3] The reduction of error in the fitted model is about 8 percent better than the null model and the chi-square is significant at the .001 level. Combined these statistics indicate that the model performs relatively well. Ten variables of substantive interest are statistically significant at the .05 level or better.

In this area of law, both justice ideology and ideological distance are statistically significant predictors of votes on the case merits. In this way, the results support both an attitudinal and separation-of-powers explanation of judicial review. Liberal justices were found to be more likely to invalidate conservative workers' compensation statutes, but only up to a point. When the preferences of these justices reach a certain threshold, willingness to invalidate these statutes is diminished.

Figure 5.4 illustrates the conditional effects of ideological distance and justice ideology on a VOCP. The figure demonstrates the impact of these variables is essentially cancelled out by each other for most justices. Starting at zero, a movement from the left to right along the X-axis indicates that the average justice is more liberal than the other branches of government. If these justices perceive ideological distance as a threatening situation, the likelihood of invalidating a conservative statute should be significantly reduced. Results seem to support this expectation.

Table 5.7.

Stage II Probit Analysis of Individual Justice's Vote to Overturn Conservative Policy (VOCP) Regarding Workers' Compensation Laws, 1970–93

Variable	Model with Selection Process			Model Without Selection Process			Expectation
	coefficient	s.e.	z	coefficient	s.e.	z	
Justice Ideology	.006	.002	2.79**	.006	.002	2.79**	$\beta>0$
Ideological Distance	-.006	.002	-2.61**	-.006	.002	-2.59**	$\beta<0$
Divided Government	.395	.090	4.25***	.381	.092	4.12***	$\beta>0$
Amendment Difficulty	-.005	.091	-.54	-.053	.093	-.57	$\beta>0$
Method of Retention	1.790	.391	4.57***	1.750	.391	4.47***	$\beta>0$
Term Length	-1.150	.347	-3.33	-1.110	.347	-3.20***	$\beta>0$
Independent State Grounds	.110	.100	1.10	.106	.099	1.06	$\beta>0$
Standard of Review	.469	.115	4.07***	.477	.115	4.13***	$\beta>0$
Lower Court Invalidates Statute	.401	.126	3.16***	.390	.126	3.08***	$\beta>0$
Lower Court Does Not Participate	-.320	.098	-3.26***	-.326	.098	-3.33***	N. E.
Third Parties	.965	.102	9.43	.958	.102	9.39***	$\beta>0$
Benefit Eligibility	.938	.113	8.30	.939	.112	8.32***	$\beta>0$
Constant	.121	.080	1.51*	-1.98	.162	-12.26***	N. E.
IMR: Selection Variable	-2.157	.199	-10.84***	—	—	—	N. E.
Percent Correctly Predicted	91.47			89.12			
Percent Modal Category	83.62			83.62			
Reduction of Error	7.85			5.50			
Chi-Square	234.83 (13)***			230.17 (12)***			
Number of Observations	1478			1478			

NOTE: Regressing the estimated residuals against time, state, and judge dummy variables tested unit effects. Only the unit effects that were statistically significant were included in the models (i.e, none).

N.E. indicates no expectation for this variable and s.e., is the standard error.

***p ≤ .01, **p ≤ .05, *p ≤ .10, one-tailed test.

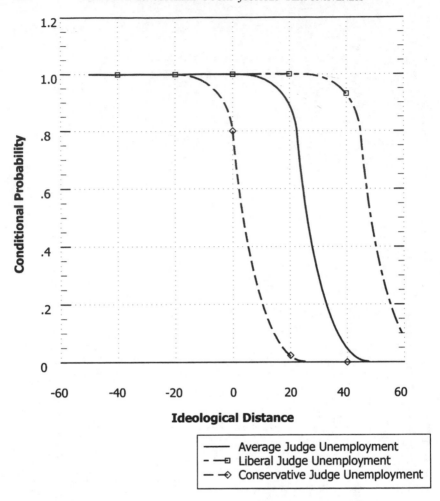

Fig. 5.4. The Conditional Effects of Distance and Judge Ideology on the Probability of Voting to Invalidate a Conservative Workers' Compensation Law, Assuming a Prior Probability of .50

However, ideological distance does not change the behavior for most justices at a prior probability of .50. Neither justices with an average ideology score nor justices with a liberal ideology score (i.e., one standard deviation above the mean) seem to reference governmental preferences when voting in these cases. Moreover, conservative justices are less likely to invalidate a conservative statute regardless of the preferences of other government actors. In this area of law, an attitudinal model of voting to invalidate statutes seems operative, at least in part.

Results from this stage also indicate that more direct policy considerations influence the behavior of individual justices when deciding these cases. Divided government is positive and statistically significant at the .05 level. Concern about policy retaliation seems to motivate justices and influence the likelihood of voting to invalidate state law.

Electoral fears also contribute to the actions of justices. Protected justices engage in adversarial behavior more by invalidating statutes. When justices are insulated from legislative or gubernatorial retention, they are significantly more likely to invalidate a conservative statute. However, term length is inversely related to the likelihood of a VOCP. The dynamics of this relationship warrant further examination.

Case facts and other elements of a legal explanation for judicial decision making seem to work well in this area of law. Standard of review is significantly and positively related to the likelihood of a VOCP. As expected, justices are more likely to invalidate the law when they evaluate the constitutionality of the statute using a strict scrutiny test. Also, when the lower court invalidates the statute, state supreme court justices are more likely to follow suit. When lower courts are not involved, however, state supreme court justices are less likely to invalidate statutes. In these instances, the state supreme court was either first to hear the case or the litigant did not raise the issue prior to reaching the court of last resort.

Finally, consider the impact of case facts on justices' votes on the constitutionality of workers' compensation statutes. Results indicate that when the statute denied benefits to the wife of a deceased husband or to the parents of a fatally injured son or daughter, justices are significantly more likely to invalidate the statute. These statutes seem to have invoked sympathy votes from justices. Also, as expected, justices are more likely to invalidate a statute that excluded certain occupations or injuries from receiving workers' compensation benefits. Typically, these statutes created economic classifications to determine the eligibility of recipients.

The Selection Process for Workers' Compensation Law

Unlike the agenda-setting stage for campaign and election law, the selection process for workers' compensation does not seem to matter in stage two of the analysis. This is not to say that there is nothing to be learned by studying agenda-setting in workers' compensation. Rather, weak statistical support for the IMR selection variable (.10 level) indicates case selection in this area of law is random or near random. Stated differently, the agenda-setting process in this area of law does not provide evidence of a selection bias. This might be because the judges are acting less strategically in these cases. Another explanation might be that case selection in this area of law is more complex, warranting future examination.

Summary of Results for Workers' Compensation Law

As found in campaign and election cases, concerns about policy retaliation seem to influence judges when deciding workers' compensation cases. However, unlike campaign and election laws, ideological distance did not significantly influence court dockets. Moreover, the effect of ideological distance on voting to invalidate the statute, under certain conditions, was counteracted by sincere preferences. In this area of law, state supreme court judges act as if ideological distance does not create a threatening situation.

Other noteworthy findings are the importance of case facts and legal doctrine in this area of law. Perhaps this is not surprising given that these issues are not as politically important to the elected members of the other branches of government. However, judges might be using factors such as standard of review or lower court involvement strategically. These relationships warrant further examination. Overall, results indicate that rewards and punishments associated with this area of law seem to pale in comparison to the political repercussions of campaign and election law. Presumably, judges have fewer reasons to engage in strategic behavior, at least in response to legislatures and governors.

UNEMPLOYMENT COMPENSATION LAW

Results for Stage I: Unemployment Compensation Law

Table 5.8 presents findings for the agenda-setting stage in unemployment compensation cases. The chi-square is statistically significant at the .001 level, indicating that the fitted model performs better than the null. The reduction of error for this model is 2.4 percent.

State supreme court judges in this area of law reveal no significant responsiveness to the preferences of other government actors. Stated differently, ideological distance neither encourages nor discourages judicial review of unemployment legislation. This finding would suggest that state supreme court justices do not perceive ideological distance as threatening in this area of law. Nor do judges perceive these instances of incongruity as opportunities to expand their role in the policymaking arena.

Results also indicate that more direct policy and electoral goals shape judicial behavior. When institutional rules make it difficult for the legislature and governor to amend the constitution, state supreme court judges are more

Table 5.8.

Stage I Probit Analysis of Docketed Judicial Review Cases (DJRC):
Constitutional Challenges to Unemployment Compensation Laws, 1970–93

Variable	coefficient	s.e.	z	Expectation
Ideological Distance	.001	.006	.17	$\beta < 0$
Divided Government	.146	.180	.81	$\beta > 0$
Amendment Difficulty	.943	.200	4.72***	$\beta > 0$
Method of Retention	.339	.258	1.39*	$\beta > 0$
Term Length	.673	.249	2.70**	$\beta > 0$
Intermediate Appellate Court	.115	.179	.64	$\beta > 0$
Constitutional Rights	−.111	.210	−.53	$\beta > 0$
Income Spent on	.003	.001	2.22**	$\beta > 0$
Unemployment Compensation				
Benefits				
Personal Income	−1.07	.040	−2.70**	$\beta < 0$
Hazard Probability	.092	.042	2.21**	N. E.
Constant	−185.200		−2.27**	N. E.
		82.435		
Percent Modal Category				96.84
Percent Correctly Predicted				97.6
Reduction of Error				2.40
Chi-square				51.37(13)***
Number of Observations				1200

NOTE: Regressing the estimated residuals against time, state, and region dummy variables tested unit effects. Only the unit effects that were statistically significant were included in the models (i. e., southern states, midwestern states and northeastern states).

N.E. indicates no expectation for this variable and s.e., is the standard error. UC indicates unemployment compensation.

***$p \leq .01$, **$p \leq .05$, *$p \leq .10$, one-tailed test.

likely to resolve constitutional challenges to these statutes. Table 5.9 presents the marginal effects of the statically significant variables on the likelihood of a DJRC challenging legislation in this area of law. As before, these effects were estimated using the sample mean as the baseline probability (.11) with other variables held constant. In these states, the probability of a case being on the state supreme court docket is increased by almost 4 percent compared to states where it is easier to amend the state constitution.

Table 5.9 also illustrates that retention methods and length of term significantly increase the likelihood of a DJRC. In states with longer terms,

Table 5.9.
Marginal Effects for Stage I Probit Analysis: The Likelihood of a DJRC on Unemployment Compensation

Variable	All	No Distance	Low Distance	High Distance	No Intermediate Appellate Court	Intermediate Appellate Court	Short Term Length	Not Retained by Legislature or Governor	Easy to Amend	Difficult to Amend
Ideological Distance	N.S.	N.S.	N.S.	N.S.	N.S.	N.S.	N.S.	N.S.	N.S.	N.S.
Divided Government	N.S.	N.S.	N.S.	N.S.	N.S.	N.S.	N.S.	N.S.	N.S.	N.S.
Amendment Difficulty	.0350	.0304	.0299	.0442	.0389	.0332	.0319	.0356	—	—
Method of Retention	.0126	.0109	.0107	.0159	.0140	.0119	—	—	.0061	.0333
Term Length	.0250	.0217	.0213	.0315	.0277	.0237	.0226	.0252	.0121	.0660
Intermediate Appellate Court	N.S.	N.S.	N.S.	N.S.	N.S.	N.S.	N.S.	N.S.	N.S.	N.S.
Constitutional Rights	N.S.	N.S.	N.S.	N.S.	N.S.	N.S.	N.S.	N.S.	N.S.	N.S.
Income Spent on Unemployment Compensation Benefits	.0310	.0270	.0260	.0390	.0290	.0340	.0290	.0320	.0310	.0320
Personal Income	−.0400	−.0350	−.0340	−.0510	−.0380	−.0450	−.0400	−.0380	−.0470	−.0420

NOTE: Marginal effects for each variable are computed when all other variables are at their means or modal categories. Modal categories are as follows: intermediate appellate court, divided government, not retained by legislature or governor, easy-to-amend state constitution, short-term length, and states without certain constitutionally protected rights. Means are as follows: ideological distance, 10.41, Personal Income, 10, 305.51, and Unemployment Compensation (UC) Benefits, 8.79.

N.S. indicates not statistically significant and thus indistinguishable from zero.

the probability of having a DJRC, challenging unemployment legislation, increases by 2.5 percent compared to states with below average term lengths.

Unlike workers' compensation cases, contextual variables such as money spent on unemployment benefits and personal income significantly influence the likelihood of a DJRC challenging an unemployment compensation statute. The probability of having a DJRC challenging an unemployment statute is 4 percent higher in wealthier states compared to poorer states. Additionally, states that spend a higher proportion of their resources on unemployment compensation are 3.1 percent more likely to have cases resolving challenges to unemployment statutes on state supreme court dockets. The supply of and demand for unemployment compensation significantly shapes court dockets.

Similar to workers' compensation cases, but unlike campaign and elections, the presence of an intermediate appellate court and constitutionally protected rights are not significantly related to court dockets. Beyond more direct policy and electoral threats, the agenda-setting process for this area of law seems to play to the economic forces operating in the states. This finding also comports with earlier work, which found similar state characteristics related to the aggregate docket of state supreme courts (Atkins and Glick 1976).

Results for Stage II: Unemployment Compensation Law

Once again attention turns to votes of the justices when they decide constitutional challenges to unemployment compensation laws. In this stage, 212 votes for 121 different state supreme court justices are examined. Table 5.10 presents the results for the likelihood of a justice casting a vote to overturn a conservative policy (i.e., VOCP).[4] The performance of the model is much better in this stage than in the agenda-setting stage. The reduction of error in the fitted model is 10 percent better than the null model, indicating that the fitted model is more appropriate than the null. Also, the chi-square is significant at the .001 level. Moreover, most of the variables of substantive interest are statistically significant at the .05 level or better and receive directional support.

Both sincere preferences and ideological distance also are found to be statistically significant predictors of justice voting. Here again, there is support for both an attitudinal and separation-of-powers explanation of judicial review under different conditions. Figure 5.5 illustrates the conditional relationship between these two variables. Moving from left to right along the X-axis, the figure demonstrates that critical concern about legislative and gubernatorial preferences are evident only at certain levels of ideological distance. Prior to this, sincere ideologies would lead judges to overturn statutes. However, as justices become more ideologically distant from the other branches of government, they are less likely to invalidate the statute. Perhaps equally important are the threshold points at which justices alter their behavior. The

Table 5.10.

Stage II Probit Analysis of Individual Justice's Vote to Overturn Conservative Policy (VOCP) Regarding Unemployment Compensation Laws, 1970–93

	Model with Selection Process			Model Without Selection Process			Expectation
	B	s.e.	b/s.e.	B	s.e.	b/s.e.	
Justice Ideology	.097	.029	3.33***	.077	.021	3.70***	β>0
Ideological Distance	-.154	.043	-3.58***	-.123	.030	-4.07***	β<0
Divided Government	1.818	.935	1.94**	.720	.821	.88	β>0
Independent State Grounds	.125	.540	.23	.059	.497	.12	β>0
Rational Basis standard of review	.639	.925	.69	.074	.808	.09	β<0
Lower Court Invalidates Statute	1.533	.842	1.82*	1.309	.586	2.23**	β>0
Good Cause: Domestic	3.359	.723	4.65***	3.341	.667	5.00***	β>0
Work Capability	2.905	.981	2.96**	2.747	.902	3.04***	β>0
IMR: Selection Variable	-1.414	.723	-1.95**				N. E.
Constant	-9.450	2.910	-3.25**	-10.080	2.650	-3.79***	
Percent Correctly Predicted			99.06			98.11	
Percent Modal Category			89.16			89.16	
Reduction of Error			9.90			8.95	
Chi-square			102.26 (9)***			99.39 (8)***	
Number of Observations			212			212	

NOTE: Regressing the estimated residuals against time, state, and judge dummy variables tested unit effects. Only the unit effects that were statistically significant were included in the models (i.e., none).

N.E. indicates no expectation for this variable and s.e., is the standard error.

***p ≤ .01, **p ≤ .05, *p ≤ .10, one-tailed test.

graph illustrates liberal justices adhere to their sincere preferences until they reach a distance of about thirty marks from the legislature and governor. As justices move beyond an ideological distance score of thirty, they become increasingly disinclined to cast a vote to overturn these statutes.

Justices also seem to act as though the threat of policy retaliation is reduced under divided government. As in the other two areas of law, justices

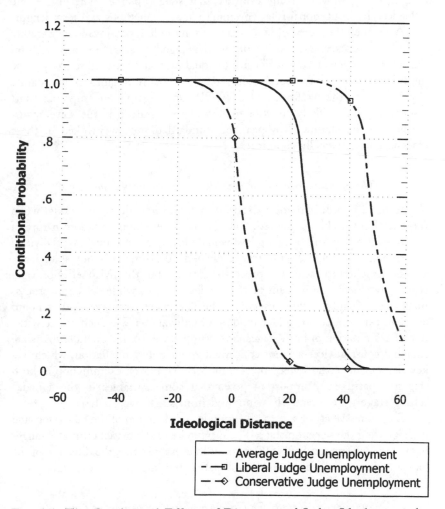

Fig. 5.5. The Conditional Effects of Distance and Judge Ideology on the Probability of Voting to Invalidate a Conservative Unemployment Compensation Law, Assuming a Prior Probability of .50

were found to be more likely to vote to invalidate statutes when the conditions in the environment make it more difficult for the legislature and governor to override a judge's preference.

States where judges are insulated from electoral retribution, however, rarely decided the fate of unemployment law. As a result, there are too few observations to make valid inferences about the impact of electoral fears on the likelihood of invalidating a statute. The fact that these variables played an important role in agenda-setting provides some evidence that state supreme court justices are influenced by institutional rules governing retention methods and term length.

As in the other areas of law, justices are more likely to invalidate a statute if it places an excessive burden on disadvantaged groups. Similarly, statutes that might be perceived as offensive to equal protection are more likely to be invalidated. The lower court's ruling on the constitutionality of the statute also influences the likelihood of a VOCP. Once again, state supreme court justices are more likely to vote to invalidate a statute if the lower court invalidated the statute. However, the standard of review invoked in these cases is not statistically significant.

The Selection Process for Unemployment Compensation Law

While there is only a modest decrease in the overall fit of the model when the selection variable is ignored, failure to consider the nonrandom nature of agenda-setting in this area of law would downplay the impact of divided government. As table 18 illustrates, divided government is not statistically significant when the selection process is ignored, but the IMR selection variable is statistically significant at the .05 level. Thus, while selection process matters only slightly with respect to the parameter estimates and standard errors in this model, our understanding of judicial review is incomplete without an examination of both stages. For example, we would conclude that state supreme court justices are not concerned about policy retaliation, which is a key element in separation-of-powers models. Moreover, examination of both stages is particularly important given that some variables in the agenda-setting stage were effectively winnowed from stage two analyses.

As before, we can assess the magnitude and direction of the bias associated with ignoring the selection stage. The magnitude of the biased estimates ranges between 5 percent and almost 90 percent. In every instance, the direction of the bias was downward, thereby underestimating the impact of these variables.

Summary of Results for Unemployment Compensation Law

Perhaps the most important finding in this area of law is that fear of policy retaliation shapes the docket and influences the likelihood that a justice will vote to invalidate state law. Rules and political situations that reduce the threat of policy retaliation thus seem to expand a judge's safety zone. Judges with more expansive safety zones seem to be more adversarial players in the policymaking arena. Equally important in this area of law are electoral incentives. When rules insulate judges from electoral retribution, reviewing statutes is much more prevalent.

WELFARE BENEFITS LAW

Results for Stage I: Welfare Benefits Law

Table 5.11 presents the results of the agenda-setting stage for welfare cases. The overall fit of the model is not very good. The reduction of error is about 2 percent, but the chi-square is statistically significant at the .001 level. Four of the substantive variables of interest are statistically significant at the .05

Table 5.11.

Stage I Probit Analysis of Docketed Judicial Review Cases (DJRC): Constitutional Challenges to Welfare Laws, 1970–93

Variable	Coefficient	s.e.	z	Expectation
Ideological Distance	.010	.005	1.91**	$\beta<0$
Divided Government	.309	.167	1.86**	$\beta>0$
Amendment Difficulty	.104	.167	.62	$\beta>0$
Method of Retention	.210	.242	.87	$\beta>0$
Term Length	.352	.209	1.68**	$\beta>0$
Intermediate Appellate Court	−.073	.177	−.41	$\beta>0$
Constitutional Rights	.367	.177	2.07**	$\beta>0$
AFDC Spending	.002	.002	.69	$\beta>0$
Hazard Probability	−.019	.013	−1.48*	N. E.
Constant	12.509		.49	N. E.
		25.429		
Reduction of Error				1.82
Percent Modal Category				97.42
Percent Correctly Predicted				97.89
Chi-square				17.22 (11)**
Number of Observations				1200

NOTE: Regressing the estimated residuals against time, state, and region dummy variables tested unit effects. Only the unit effects that were statistically significant were included in the models (i. e., southern states, northeastern states).

N.E. indicates no expectation for this variable and s.e., is the standard error.

***$p \leq .01$, **$p \leq .05$, *$p \leq .10$, one-tailed test.

level and receive directional support. The substantive impact of statistically significant variables is assessed by estimating the marginal effects at the sample mean in this area of law (.24), holding other variables constant.

Perhaps the most intriguing finding in this area of law is that ideological distance significantly increases the likelihood of a DJRC challenging a welfare law. Figure 5.6 illustrates a positive and linear effect of ideological distance on the probability of a DJRC challenging a welfare law. Recall that when judge preferences are out-of-sync with legislative and gubernatorial preferences in campaign and election cases, reviewing statutes was inhibited. In this area of law, the opposite is true. The result comports with the expectations of this project; forces influencing judicial review should be different across areas of law of varying degrees of political detriment to the elected elite.

As expected, divided government also exerts a significant effect on the likelihood of a DJRC. As Table 5.12 illustrates, the probability of a DJRC

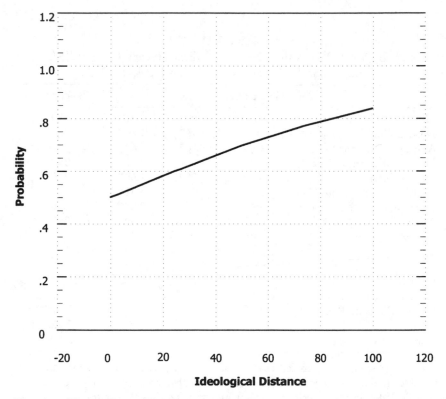

Fig. 5.6. The Effects of Ideological Distance on the Probability of a DJRC Challenging a Welfare Law, Assuming a Prior Probability of .50

Table 5.12.
Marginal Effects for Stage I Probit Analysis: The Liklihood of a DJRC on Welfare Benefits

Variable	All	No Distance	Low Distance	High Distance	No Intermediate Appellate Court	Intermediate Appellate Court	Short Term Length	Not Retained by Legislature or Governor	Easy to Amend	Difficult to Amend
Ideological Distance	.0177	—	—	—	.0147	.0177	.0147	.0177	.0147	.0206
Divided Government	.0165	.0118	.0142	.0245	.0146	.0175	.0135	.0171	.0145	.0200
Amendment Difficulty	N.S.	N.S.	N.S.	N.S.	N.S.	N.S.	N.S.	N.S.	N.S.	N.S.
Method of Retention	N.S.	N.S.	N.S.	N.S.	N.S.	N.S.	N.S.	N.S.	N.S.	N.S.
Term Length	.0122	.0088	.0106	.0182	.0108	.0130	.0101	.0127	.0108	.0149
Intermediate Appellate Court	N.S.	N.S.	N.S.	N.S.	N.S.	N.S.	N.S.	N.S.	N.S.	N.S.
Constitutional Rights	N.S.	N.S.	N.S.	N.S.	N.S.	N.S.	N.S.	N.S.	N.S.	N.S.
AFDC Spending	N.S.	N.S.	N.S.	N.S.	N.S.	N.S.	N.S.	N.S.	N.S.	N.S.

NOTE: Marginal effects for each variable are computed when all other variables are at their means or modal categories. Modal categories are as follows: intermediate appellate court, divided government, not retained by legislature or governor, easy-to-amend state consitution, short-term length, and states without certain constitutionally protected rights. Means are as follows: distance, 10.41 and AFDC Spending, 3.94.

N.s. indicates not statistically significant and thus indistinguishable from zero.

challenging a welfare law is about 2 percent higher under divided government than when government is unified. Examination of this relationship across various levels of ideological distance also is informative. When ideological distance is one standard deviation above average, states with divided government are 2.4 percent more likely to have a DJRC challenging a welfare law compared to when there is unified government. Fear of policy retaliation, however, does not seem to matter with respect to difficulty in amending state constitutions.

Electoral considerations play a mixed role in shaping the court's agenda. In states with longer terms, the probability of a DJRC challenging a welfare law is about 1.2 percent higher than in states where judges have short terms. The impact of term length on the likelihood of reviewing statutes also varies positively as ideological distance increases. However, method of retention is not statistically significant in this area of law.

Results also show states that have constitutionally protected rights to privacy, equal protection, and/or right to vote are significantly more likely to have a DJRC challenging welfare legislation. However, the presence of an intermediate appellate court does not shape the docket of state supreme courts in this area. Moreover, state welfare demand does not significantly influence the presence of these cases on state supreme court dockets.

Results for Stage II: Welfare Benefits Law

In this stage, one hundred sixty-three individual votes for ninety-three different justices are evaluated. The dependent variable is the likelihood that a justice will vote to overturn a conservative policy (VOCP). The model performs reasonably well, with a 10 percent reduction of error. The chi-square is also statistically significant at the .001 level. Both of these statistics indicate the model performs significantly better than the null. Eight of the variables of substantive interest are also statistically significant and receive directional support (see table 5.13).

Judge ideology and ideological distance are both statistically significant predictors of voting behavior. The likelihood of a VOCP varies positively with sincere preferences and inversely with ideological distance. As before, the impact of these variables on VOCP in terms of conditional probabilities is considered.

Figure 5.7 shows that individual justices become increasingly concerned about the preferences of the other branches of government. However, the figure also illustrates that justices are not always compelled to follow the preferences of other governmental actors. Conservative justices who are most distant from the other branches of government (i.e., at a distance of 40), for example, are least likely to invalidate conservative laws. Thus, in some

Table 5.13.
Stage II Probit Analysis of Individual Justice's Vote to Overturn Conservative Policy (VOCP) Regarding Welfare Benefit Laws, 1970–93

Variable	Model with Selection Process			Model Without Selection Process			Expectation
	coefficient	s.e.	z	coefficient	s.e.	z	
Justice Ideology	.054	.016	3.28***	.049	.013	3.68***	$\beta>0$
Ideological Distance	−.093	.027	−3.43***	−.086	.022	−3.90***	$\beta<0$
Divided Government	1.379	.596	2.31**	1.459	.582	2.51**	$\beta>0$
Amendment Difficulty	1.327	.691	1.92**	.721	.590	1.22	$\beta>0$
Method of Retention	.751	.791	.95	.569	.779	.73	$\beta>0$
Term Length	2.477	.872	2.84**	1.570	.657	2.39**	$\beta>0$
Independent State Grounds	.772	.525	1.47*	.882	.569	1.55*	$\beta>0$
Rational basis standard of review	−1.335	.473	−2.82**	−1.402	.475	−2.95**	$\beta<0$
Lower Court Invalidates Law	1.454	.746	1.95**	1.641	.662	2.48**	$\beta>0$
Lower Court Does Not Participate	.149	.781	.19	.043	.708	.06	N. E.
Residency Requirement	.297	.596	.50	.495	.584	.85	$\beta>0$
Constant	2.374	1.410	1.68**	−7.242	1.830	−3.96	N. E.
IMR: Selection Variable	−13.153	4.574	−2.87	—	—	—	N. E.
Percent Correctly Predicted	92.54			87.57			
Percent Modal Category	82.60			82.60			
Reduction of Error	9.95			4.97			
Chi-square	68.62 (13)***			63.71 (12)***			
Number of Observations	163			163			

NOTE: Regressing the estimated residuals against time, state, and judge dummy variables tested unit effects. Only the unit effects that were statistically significant were included in the models (i.e., none).

N.E. indicates no expectation for this variable and s.e., is the standard error.

***$p \leq .01$, **$p \leq .05$, *$p \leq .10$, one-tailed test.

instances, as was the situation in unemployment cases, justices have incentive to reference the other branches of government when voting. Stated more simply, ideological distance seems to inhibit adversarial behavior.

As was found in stage one and across the other three areas of law, state supreme court justices seem very attuned to threats of policy retaliation. Both divided government and amendment difficulty significantly and predictably

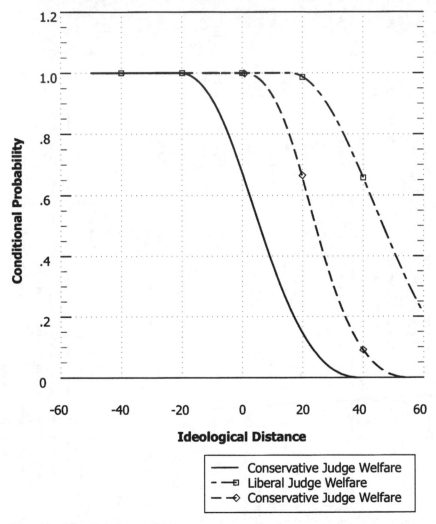

Fig. 5.7. The Conditional Effects of Ideological Distance and Judge Ideology on the Probability of Voting to Invalidate a Welfare Law, Assuming a Prior Probability of .50

influence the likelihood of a VOCP. Term length also was found to exert a statistically significant effect in this area of law. In these instances, justices were significantly more likely to intervene.

Legal and case characteristics also influence voting in this area of law. As expected, state supreme court justices are significantly less likely to invalidate a statute when it was subjected to the rational basis test. Once again, the lower court's ruling on the constitutionality of the statute mattered. When lower court judges invalidate the statute, state supreme court justices also are more likely to invalidate the statute. Type of statute was not statistically significant in this area of law.

The Selection Process for Welfare Benefits Law

The selection process in stage one is significantly related to stage two of this analysis. The IMR selection variable is statistically significant, and two important differences are observed. First, the reduction of error drops to about half (4.9 percent) in the model without the selection variable. Second, and perhaps more important, ignoring the selection process downplays the impact of institutional rules on voting behavior. If we were to exclude the selection variable from the model, or focus attention solely on the vote on the merits, we would conclude that electoral contingencies do not impinge on state supreme court justice behavior.

The magnitude of the bias with respect to the parameter estimates ranges between a positive 66 percent to a negative 71 percent. Not only does the model ignoring case selection produce inefficient standard errors for the variables associated with electoral retribution, but the model also produced biased estimates for these variables. In this area of law, the impact of case facts was overestimated by 66 percent, leading one to think case facts play a much more prominent role in the decision on the merits when in reality the impact is quite modest compared to the other variables. The impact of divided government also is overestimated by 6 percent in this model. Here again, the story seems to be very similar to the other areas of law; agenda-setting influences the decision on the merits.

Summary of Results for Welfare Benefits Law

In this area of law, as expected, court dockets are less responsive to strategic considerations in their external political environment. The agenda-setting stage does not seem to be influenced by differences in institutional rules governing the retention process of state supreme court judges. However, policy and electoral goals significantly and predictably influence the likelihood that a justice will vote to overturn a statute.

GENERAL COMMENTS ACROSS ALL FOUR AREAS OF LAW

Clearly other factors beyond separation-of-powers and attitudinal explanations are shaping the dockets of state supreme courts and influencing the voting behavior of justices. The separation-of-powers conceptualization of the policymaking process speaks directly to policy retaliatory mechanisms; yet, an important feature of state political systems is that judges also confront electoral constraints.

Chapter Six

Conclusion: Independence and Accountability in State Supreme Courts

As chapter five demonstrated, whether state supreme court justices vote sincerely or strategically depends upon: (1) the ideological difference between justices and other state government actors; (2) the degree to which institutional rules and designs, and political settings shield judges from retaliation against judges for objectionable decisions; and most fundamentally (3) the area of law. Within an ideological "safety zone," justices' preferences are similar to those of other government actors such that strategic voting is not required. Some rules and settings also create "safety zones," shielding justices from retaliation and encouraging sincere behavior. Whether justices vote sincerely or strategically outside of this safety zone depends on the area of law.

Since institutional rules do not vary for the United States Supreme Court but do for the fifty states, state supreme court cases are the best site for testing conditions under which justices are likely to vote strategically. Using data on docketing and decisions regarding the constitutional fate of four areas of law from 1970–1993, this research demonstrates that the likelihood of strategic behavior by judges varies by preference distributions, divided party control of state governments, constitutional amendment procedures, judicial retention practices, length of judicial terms, and degree of saliency associated with the area of law.

Fundamentally, results from these analyses demonstrate that state supreme court justices vote sincerely when the feel they can and strategically when they feel they must. Clearly, state supreme court justices do not operate as singularly powerful policymaking actors whose decisions are insulated from external constraints. Overall, justices are significantly less likely to review and invalidate statutes when justices act outside of the safety zone. Justices acting in less threatening environments are more likely to docket constitutional challenges and invalidate laws.

These findings support research by Brace and Hall (e.g., 1995, 1997) and Brace, Hall, and Langer (1999, 2001) that demonstrate judicial preferences, institutional rules, and political contexts shape judicial incentives in state supreme courts (See also Langer 1997). Results also support Jeffrey A. Segal's (1997) most recent evidence regarding sincere behavior by Supreme Court Justices. Justices sitting on courts in the American states that most resemble the insularity afforded to the United States Supreme Court behave like members on that Court, according to their sincere preferences. However, areas of law that have few political repercussions for legislatures and governors also promote sincere behavior, irrespective of rules and ideological distance.

Results also demonstrate the importance of examining both stages of judicial review if we are to gain a more complete understanding of the conditions under which state supreme court justices act strategically. Essentially, in salient areas of law, judges seemed to exercise gate-keeping powers in hopes of reducing political vulnerabilities in the next stage. Stated differently, justices seemingly avoid rendering constitutional decisions in cases that might increase the likelihood of retaliation. Conversely, these judges act as if they are willing to decide (and subsequently invalidate) constitutional challenges to laws when the policy area is of little or no concern to the other branches of government.

COMPARATIVE ASSESSMENT OF STATE JUDICIAL REVIEW

The findings suggest that strategic behavior does occur, but how much and what are the most prominent reasons? To address these questions, I assay the results across different areas of law, generalizing them to judicial behavior in the policymaking game. I also weigh the evidence with respect to some of the conceptualizations of judicial behavior and assess their applicability in state supreme courts. An audit of these findings will illustrate insights gained from a systematic comparative inquiry of judicial review in both stages of this process and across multiple areas of law.

First, we can assess the magnitudes and combinations of forces influencing behavior at both stages of judicial review to assess the degree of strategic behavior exhibited in each area of law. Strategic behavior would be most evidenced when the magnitude of the relationship between the indicators for policy and electoral constraints and judicial review is strong (i.e., larger coefficient) and justices predictably and significantly shift their behavior as if they are responding to retaliatory fears. When behaving strategically, these judges will be less likely to intervene in stage one and invalidate the law in stage two.

Alternatively, sincere behavior is evidenced when the size of the coefficients for the indicators of policy and electoral constraints are small. In these instances, state supreme courts act as if they are not concerned about policy or electoral threats; state supreme court justices should be more likely to intervene and invalidate laws. Assessing the magnitudes of the coefficients on divided government, difficulty in amendment procedure, method of retention, and term length thus offers a ranking of strategic behavior across areas of law.

Institutional rules, judicial preferences, the preferences of the legislature and governor, legal doctrine, case facts, and other external factors were all found to be significant predictors of reviewing and invalidating state statutes, but the impact varied by area of law (see Table 6.1). The results across the four areas demonstrate the centrality of institutions in both the agenda-setting stage and decision-on-the-merits stage; institutional rules were the most consistent predictors of behavior in each area of law. One benefit of comparative inquiry is that it allows us to assess the magnitude of the relationships across a multitude of issues, judges, and settings. Subsequently I highlight some of the general findings in terms of the magnitude of the coefficients in these models.

Justices seemingly are most strategic when reviewing challenges to campaign and election laws. In these cases, the impact of ideological distance was most pronounced and inversely related to the likelihood of court intervention. Divided government, difficulty in amendment procedure, and method of judicial retention also are very strong indicators of judicial behavior in these cases. On the other hand, state supreme court justices appeared less strategic when deciding the fate of welfare legislation. Overwhelmingly in these cases, justices acted as if they were unconcerned by potential retaliatory actions of the other branches of government. When institutional rules and political context afford judges latitude in these welfare cases, judicial behavior was supportive of an attitudinal explanation. For example, ideological distance in these cases increased the likelihood of intervention and justice's preferences played most prominently in the decision on the merits.

Workers' compensation and unemployment compensation cases fall somewhere in-between strategic and sincere behavior in terms of overall results and in comparison to the other areas of law. Workers' compensation more closely exhibits strategic behavior whereas unemployment compensation cases tend to be docketed and decided more on the basis of sincere preferences. However, the issue of paid family leave, which is being considered as part of unemployment compensation programs, has moved to the front line of state legislative politics. According to the NCSL, legislatures in fifteen states

Table 6.1.
Summary of Results Across Four Areas of Law

	Campaign and Election Laws		Workers' Compensation Laws		Unemployment Compensation Laws		Welfare Benefit Laws	
	Agenda Setting	Vote on Merits	Agenda Setting	Vote on Merits	Agenda Setting	Vote on Merits	Agenda Setting	Vote on Merits
Justice Ideology (sincere)	—	YES	—	YES	—	YES	YES	YES
Policy Threat—Ideological Distance	YES	NO	NO	YES	NO	YES	YES	YES
Policy Threat—Divided Government or Amendment Difficulty	YES	YES	YES	YES	YES	YES	YES	YES
Not Retained by Legislature or Governor or Short Term Length	YES	YES	YES	YES	YES	YES	YES	YES
Contextual	YES	—	NO	—	YES	—	NO	—
Other Institutional	YES	—	NO	—	NO	—	YES	—
Legal and Case Facts	—	YES	—	YES	—	YES	—	YES
Selection	—	YES	—	NO	—	YES	—	YES

NOTE: Yes indicates at least one of the variables in the category had a statically significant impact on the likelihood of reviewing or invalidating state statutes. Significance is measured at the .05 level or better.

introduced bills to fund birth and adoption leave with unemployment insurance surtaxes in 2000. This might raise the stakes for unemployment compensation, sparking heated battles in this area of law and expanding the scope of conflict. As a result, future examinations of unemployment laws might show considerably more strategic behavior on the part of judges.

Overall, it seems that areas of law most salient to the other branches of government are likely to encourage the most strategic behavior, under certain conditions. Instead of serving as a countermajoritarian institution, when the issue resonates most with other branches of government state supreme court justices avoid getting involved in the first place. Judges rarely intervene and when they do, they are more likely to uphold the law. Hence, when the issues are near and dear to the legislature and governor, the legislature and governor serve as the final arbiters of public policy. Conversely, in areas of law where the issues were less salient to the other branches of government, justices voted in accordance with their sincere ideology. The final arbiters of welfare and unemployment legislation in the American states seem to be state supreme court justices, at least in the short run.

Theoretical Contributions and Substantive Implications

A comparative assessment of the magnitude of the relationships across models also demonstrates the limitations of a pure attitudinal or pure separation-of-powers explanation. This comparative inquiry has demonstrated that under the right set of conditions, state supreme court justices are active participants in the policymaking process, voting according to ideology. Judicial preferences therefore play an important role in some areas of public policy in the American states.

Attitudes, however, only account for some of the behavior. Results indicated that judicial review of campaign and election laws was overwhelmingly shaped by variables measuring prospective policy retaliation. State supreme court justices acted as if the legislature and governor would override their decision. Thus, judges are seemingly worried about policy retaliation when they are not in-sync with the other branches of government (i.e., ideologically distant), *and* the issue is highly salient to these other government actors. However, when judges are in sync with the other branches of government, they act as if they are indifferent with respect to reviewing these cases and invalidating legislation.

A separation-of-powers model that posits fear of policy retaliation will curtail judicial activism only works well in campaign and election cases. In workers' compensation, unemployment compensation and welfare cases, electoral concerns and other institutional and contextual forces outweigh policy considerations. In these cases, especially welfare, state supreme court justices were considerably more likely to intervene. Fear of policy retaliation seems to influence behavior, but in these areas of law, policy ambitions tell only part of the story. Adding electoral concerns to the picture moves us closer to a more complete understanding of judicial review.

From a jurisprudential perspective, legal doctrine and case facts should influence judicial review. A relatively consistent finding across the four areas of law was that lower court invalidation of a statue significantly increased the likelihood that a state supreme court justice would invalidate the statute. However, consistency between the lower court and state supreme courts also has a strategic overtone. S. Sidney Ulmer (1983, 1984) has demonstrated, intercircuit conflict is an important variable in predicting cases that make it on the United States Supreme Court's docket. Extending this logic to the American states (see, e.g., Baum 1979), consistency between state courts may simply be a way of thwarting intervention by a higher court. Stated differently, harmony among the state courts on a particular issue might preserve the state supreme court's status as final arbiter of state policy. However, the impact of legal doctrine and case facts was most evident in welfare cases and least evident in campaign and elections.

Overall, the impact of legal factors varies by area of law and in most cases does not provide a convincing explanation of judicial review. State supreme court justices are not simply followers or "interpretators" of the law, but rather innovative policymakers who under some circumstances and in certain areas of law act as if they are basing decisions on factors that go beyond legal doctrine or the facts of the case. Fundamentally, judges often are basing their votes on the anticipated reaction of the legislature and governor.

What is perhaps not too surprising, especially given the wealth of evidence, is that institutional rules and political conditions dictate the extent to which judges respond to either electoral or policy threats, as well as internal legal stimuli. One observation is that when the area of law summons many more actors to the arena with greater stakes in the game, such as campaign and elections and workers' compensation, strategic explanations of judicial behavior seem to be at play. To the extent that sincere behavior protects minority interests, when the area of law involves participants less capable of effective mobilization (e.g., welfare recipients), justices protect the underdog.

Methodological Implications

Some observations about both stages of judicial review and in particular the selection process are important. The comparisons across models within each area of law also demonstrate that in three areas of law stage two was fundamentally tied to the agenda-setting processes for state supreme courts. As a result, the conclusions drawn about state supreme court justices and their policymaking function via judicial review are incomplete unless both stages of the process are considered. Perhaps more importantly, an understanding of strategic behavior is hampered when the nonrandom nature of agenda-setting is omitted from the analysis. Douglas G. Baird, Robert H. Gertner, and Randal M. Picker (1994) note "that, . . . legal analysts commonly draw inferences about legal rules from a study of litigated cases. In order to draw the correct inferences from such a study, however, it is important to know the extent to which the few cases that are litigated differ systematically from all the disputes that arise. If these suits are not representative of the population of disputes, and they most certainly are not, one must take account of the selection effect, which might also influence the way judges decide cases" (206).

A comparison of the differences in the results, with and without the selection processes modeled, demonstrate the limitations of ignoring the agenda-setting stage when studying the decision-on-the-merits stage. For example, electoral constraints were underestimated in three of the four areas of law by a range of 3 to 48 percent. Equally troubling is that in welfare and unemployment cases the estimated impact of judicial preferences was underestimated. Moreover, in some instances, important factors that influenced the docketing of cases were not found to be significant variables in the vote on the merits; the influence of these factors essentially was most at play in the first stage and thus had a lesser impact on stage two. Examination of only one stage thus ignores important processes that can enhance or mitigate the need to behave strategically.

Overall, many of the parameter estimates for all four areas of law were biased when the selection process was ignored. Of these estimates about 35 percent had inefficient standard errors. The results in this book clearly demonstrate the necessity to examine both stages of judicial review if we want a more complete and accurate understanding of the conditions under which judges on these courts will make policy through the power of judicial review.

IMPLICATIONS OF JUDICIAL REVIEW
ON DEMOCRATIC PRINCIPLES

This study has addressed some fundamental questions about the role of state supreme court justices in the policymaking arena. More broadly, this research has sought to understand judicial review in two fundamental stages of the process: (1) agenda-setting, and (2) decision-on-the-merits. While the literature discussed in chapter one provided some evidence that state supreme courts engage in judicial review, these courts have oscillated between interventionists and restrained actors in the policymaking arena. Moreover, the literature on judicial review indicates that this court function was traditionally used as a way to protect the judiciary against encroachments of power by other branches of government. Results from this study suggest judicial review is more often *avoided* to protect justices from retaliation by other branches of government.

Scholars (see, e.g., Sheldon 1987) have documented that since the 1970s courts have expanded their use of judicial review, particularly in areas regulating political and economic resources. To some extent this study seems to support these contentions. State supreme court justices resolved issues across a broad range of policies in the four areas of law examined. However, justices were least likely to engage in judicial review of campaign and election law when rules and conditions placed justices outside a safety zone; yet, judges were more likely to review and invalidate statutes in areas regulating economic resources, such as unemployment compensation and welfare. Judges on these benches may have expanded the use of judicial review to areas regulating political and economic resources, but they are much more cautious in the former area than in the latter. This leads to another important observation: state supreme court justices take on greater policymaking roles in areas traditionally viewed as part of the legislature's turf (i.e., issues that effect state budgets).

However, this policymaking role, for example, is tempered in areas of law that can affect state budgets when the issue involves the redistribution of monetary resources from mobilized participants (e.g., business) to less mobilized participants (e.g., injured workers). Which of the three branches of government really possess the power of the purse is in part dictated by the wherewithal of the participants likely to receive or lose benefits.

Why these courts play varying roles in the policymaking game has important implications on democratic principles. This book offers one answer, though not the only one—clearly more work needs to be done. Policy saliency and political repercussions, as conceptualized in this project, provide a better understanding of why judges are much less hesitant to review and invalidate welfare laws, for example, than campaign and election laws. The theory of judicial review across areas of law forwarded in this book also helps explain when and why judges are most likely to operate as protectors of minority rights, and when judges are more likely to uphold or protect majoritarian interests.

Election laws that discriminated against third parties, for example, were more likely to be challenged when judges were insulated from political pressures and threatening environments. Quite simply, judges when reviewing salient areas of law seem to be willing to protect the minority when these judges do not have to protect themselves from their environment. Conversely, discriminatory policies against minorities or the disadvantaged were more apt to receive harsh treatment by judges, when the area of law was less directly tied to government ambitions. Protecting the disadvantaged is a role judges take on when they are autonomous or when the policy is of little or no concern to formidable players in the policy arena.

Thus, the findings of this research can address debates, regarding consequences of constitutional design and institutional rules on public policy and majority will. Scholarly debate about the degree and nature of autonomy afforded members of the United States Supreme Court continues, but disagreement often rests on whether or not fear of policy retribution alters this Court's behavior. Perhaps Madison's constitutional design that accords each branch of government checks to counteract government ambitions failed with respect to the United States Supreme Court.

Theoretically, the constitutional design instituting separation-of-powers and checks-and-balances gave Congress and the president authority to prevent members of the judiciary from pursuing ambitions that might allow minority interests to thwart the will of the people. Empirically these checks on the judiciary seem to have more "bark than bite." This is not to say that all or any of the United States Supreme Court's actions protect the minority over the majority, but this Court seemingly has the power to do so.

Accountability mechanisms through policy sanctions are apparently not enough to curb sincere preferences of United States Supreme Court justices (see e.g., Segal 1997; Segal and Spaeth 1993; Spaeth and Segal 1999). Here, judicial protection of minority rights (or the disadvantaged) seems to be mostly linked to the ideological makeup of the bench.

Examination of judicial review across different institutional rules, political settings, and areas of law shows that protection of minorities is not always tied to judicial preferences. Should state supreme court justices want to strike down legislation that discriminates against disadvantaged persons, their preference to do so is often hindered by rules and settings that link the fate of these justices to the other branches of government or make it easier for these other government actors to repudiate judicial preferences. The need to vote strategically might indeed force justices to forgo the fights that place them in opposition with government. Often these fights are on behalf of the underdog.

Justices on our nation's highest Court often do not need to engage in strategic behavior. Attitudinalists offer essentially three reasons why justices on the United States Supreme Court rarely engage in strategic behavior. Quite simply, these justices are not electorally accountable, they do not have ambitions for higher office and their decisions are rarely overturned and not subject to a higher court of law (Spaeth 1979, 113).[1] As a result, this Court is often viewed as a uniquely powerful, highly autonomous policymaking institution. Presumably democracy entails responsiveness to popular will; yet members of the United States Supreme Court seem mostly unaccountable to the electorate, and other branches of government (Segal and Spaeth 1993; Segal 1997; Spaeth and Segal 1999, but see Mishler and Sheehan 1993, 1996; Flemming and Wood 1997).

Democratic theorists concerned about the unchecked power afforded our nation's highest Court might rest easier knowing that state supreme court justices often act as if the power of judicial review is not unchecked. When institutional rules or political conditions increase the likelihood of legislative and gubernatorial retaliation against judges, a state supreme court justice's judicial review function is highly constrained.

As Fenno (1978) astutely noted decades ago, successful pursuit of political ambitions requires awareness of constituent demands. In this book, constituents are defined as governmental actors with the authority to remove judges and overturn judges' decisions. It follows that if judges stray too far from the preferences of those to whom they are beholden, they may lose their seat on the bench or see their least preferred policy become law. This political reality seems to be most pronounced in policy areas of critical import to the constituents (i.e., legislature and governor).

Following in the tradition of earlier work on the United States Supreme Court (see, e.g., Murphy 1964, Rohde and Spaeth 1976) and state supreme courts (see, e.g., Brace and Hall 1990, 1997), this study also offers institutional rules and constitutional design as an overarching theory to explain variations in judicial review. The institutional approach taken complements both the attitudinal and separation-of-powers explanations and thus offers a more holistic view of state supreme courts in the policymaking arena. Examination of the judiciary in isolation from the other branches of government limits our understanding of judicial review.

A separation-of-powers conceptualization of the judiciary was developed primarily for examination of the United States Supreme Court, and, as a result, its fundamental argument is about policy retaliation and its primary focus is on Statutory interpretation. In this way, perhaps the greatest weakness in the separation-of-powers argument is that the explanation ignores electoral considerations and overlooks the importance of judicial review. It is thus important to expand this conceptualization of judicial behavior, bridge it with a neo-institutional approach, and apply it to relations among the branches of government when courts invoke the power of judicial review. This allows consideration other types and degrees of interconnectedness between the judiciary and other branches of government. It also permits examination of dual constraints operating on state supreme court justices (i.e., electoral and policy ambitions). This is necessary to advance a more general theory about judicial behavior. The results in this book clearly demonstrate that the duality of policy and electoral constraints in many instances severely inhibit the actions of judges. Thus, the judiciary should be conceptualized as an institution that is responsive to and autonomous from legislative and executive pressures, depending on the rules of the game, constitutional designs, political settings, and fundamentally, the area of law.

WHERE DO WE GO FROM HERE?

Hall recently observed, "Overcoming ignorance of the politics of state courts is necessary for a complete understanding of American politics and the vital role played by judicial institutions in the political process. . . . State courts can no longer be dismissed as inconsequential." (Hall 1999 138). This book demonstrates the important role state supreme court justices play in the policy arena via their power of judicial review. State supreme courts are one of three institutional players in the policymaking game. The role of the judiciary, however, can be constrained.

This book offers a broader conceptualization of the judiciary through systematic comparative analysis of two stages of judicial review by state supreme courts in an effort to better understand strategic behavior, in particular, and judicial responsiveness, more generally. After all, the separation-of-powers constitutional design is a fundamental tenet of democracy that was instituted to counteract political ambitions, both electoral and policy. Studies of the judiciary, particularly in the American states, warrant consideration of these ambitions pursued by the judiciary, especially given that only a small number of judges are afforded the unique autonomy afforded to members of the United States Supreme Court.

Some caution in the conclusions must be taken because justices might not be the only strategic players in this game. For example, this project begins with the premise that state supreme courts play only a reactionary role in the policy process. Charles R. Shipan (1997) recently found that interest groups and legislators engage in strategic behavior both in the drafting of legislation and in decisions to bring cases to court. Other research suggests the timing and occurrence of legislative adoption of abortion laws is strategic with respect to court ideology (Brace and Langer 2001). More recently, James R. Rogers (2001) demonstrated that judicial review has an important informational component that instructs judicial-legislative relations and informs legislative decisions to adopt policy.

Scholarly inquires of judicial review also should consider litigant behavior more directly in the initial stages of the process. Such studies require extensive data collection efforts, but more precise indicators of strategic behavior on behalf of litigants should be developed for the agenda-setting stage. While litigants are considered in a couple ways in this book and are viewed as an important part of the agenda-setting process, there are enough judicial review opportunities in the four areas of law examined to warrant attention focused on the court's decision over the agenda. Moreover, given that there are several cases appealed to these courts in each area of law every year, it would have been impractical to code and empirically evaluate these cases to assess litigant behavior when the fundamental argument pertained to the relationship among judges, legislatures, and governors. However, the exclusion of direct measures of litigant behavior from the selection model does not allow me to link strategic behavior to who wins in court. For example, litigants might strategize to raise constitutional challenges before courts comprised of judges who are more sympathetic to the litigant's complaint. Litigants with more where-withal and resources might be most likely and capable of strategizing. I leave these questions to future inquiry.

This study has considered policy and electoral threats anticipated directly by the primary constitutional actors in the policymaking arena, namely, the legislature and governor. In so doing, my findings can only speak indirectly to the constraints imposed by the electorate; the willingness of the legislature and governor to retaliate against judges is often linked to the public. Recall that the agenda-setting stage in workers' compensation cases was not significantly linked to the decision-on-the-merits stage in these analyses. In this area of law, case selection does not follow any systematic pattern with respect to the factors explored in this study. One reason might be that the dynamics of this policy area, and the actors involved require an examination of the preferences of additional actors (e.g., chief justice, the citizenry, and bureaucracy). Students of judicial politics should consider strategic behavior with respect to other internal and external actors.[2]

Scholars also might treat the legislature and governor as unequal partners against justices, disentangling threats levied by these actors against judges and developing more dynamic and multidimensional games. Additionally, we need to explore other goals, (see e.g., Baum 1997), different policy areas, and competing threats justices confront when engaging in judicial review. This book demonstrates conditions under which judges act strategically, and identifies the areas of law most likely and least likely to induce strategic behavior. However, more work needs to be done to evaluate motivations of judicial behavior across levels of accountability to various actors both on and off the bench. We also need more systematic examinations to assess whether strategic behavior produce outcomes that benefit the haves or the have-nots. Future studies should thus utilize similar comparative research designs to advance more general theories of judicial behavior and the relations among governmental branches.

Appendix

MEASUREMENT AND DATA SOURCES

Dependent Variable for Stage I: Agenda-Setting Stage

Equal to one in the year a state supreme court had a case on its docket in which the court ruled on the constitutionality of a statute in one of the four areas of law, zero otherwise. Cases were collected primarily using WestLaw in each of the fifty states for the 1970 through 1993 period (Lexis-Nexis was used to conduct some initial searches). Cases involving challenges to county or municipal ordinances are excluded from the analysis along with per curium decisions.

The following searches were conducted in WestLaw to identify cases in each area of law where there was a constitutional challenge to a law, and where there was a formal opinion issued:

1. TO (144) /P CONSTITUTIONAL! UNCONSTITUTIONAL! /5 STATUT! LAW PROVISION & CO (HIGH) & DA (AFT 1969 & BEF 1994) % CI (MEMO!)

2. TO (356A) /P CONSTITUTIONAL! UNCONSTITUTIONAL! /5 STATUT! LAW PROVISION & CO (HIGH) & DA (AFT 1969 & BEF 1994) % CI (MEMO!)

3. TO (413) /P CONSTITUTIONAL! UNCONSTITUTIONAL! /5 STATUT! LAW PROVISION & CO (HIGH) & DA (AFT 1969 & BEF 1994) % CI (MEMO!)

Dependent Variable for Stage II: Decision-on-the-Merits Stage

Equal to one for each justice's vote to overturn a state statute or provision, zero otherwise. Each statute was coded as liberal, conservative, or ambiguous; hence, the dependent variable was actually a vote to overturn a liberal statute or conservative statute. Some cases involved more than one statute or provision on which the court decided the constitutional fate. Each issue was treated as a separate vote. A Chow Test was conducted to see if these cases were statistically different from cases in which only one issue was before the court. There were no significant differences. Some cases also involved the participation of adjunct or temporary justices. These judges were not included in the analysis because presumably strategic considerations would not influence these judges.

CONSERVATIVE/LIBERAL POLICY:
CLASSIFICATION OF STATUTES

Campaign and Elections constituted five categories: party access to polls, voter registration, candidate qualifications, campaign disclosure, and campaign expenditures.

Conservative Statutes are those that place restrictions on the individual voter or candidate.

Liberal Statutes are those that restrict or regulate money in campaigns, such as restricting anonymous donations, or limiting amounts.

Ideologically Ambiguous Statutes are those that were not clearly associated with liberal or conservative ideologies. For example, restrictions of party access to polls, which typically involved number of signatures required for third party candidates, were included in this category.

Workers' Compensation constituted six categories: benefit calculation, benefit eligibility, benefits for third parties, attorney fees, procedural issues, civil liability, and other.

Conservative Statutes are those that prohibit certain groups from receiving benefits (e.g., firemen are not eligible for temporary total benefits, farmers are not eligible for assistance); reduce the amount of benefit received when calculating the benefit; or eliminated third parties from receiving workers' compensation (e.g., parent or spouse cannot get benefits if child or husband is fatally injured).

Liberal Statutes are those that increase the amount of benefit calculated or protects certain groups from exclusion, or expands those eligible or makes utilization or eligibility easier. There were very few statutes in this category.

Ideologically Ambiguous Statutes are those that were not clearly associated with liberal or conservative ideologies. For example, this group consisted of procedural issues, such as filing requirements; civil liability issues, such as right to sue employer or coemployee for injury in civil suit for negligence; awards attorneys fees for court proceedings; and other.

Unemployment Compensation constituted six categories: benefit calculation, work capability, good cause-other, good cause-domestic, student status, and procedural issues.

Conservative Statutes are those that prohibit certain groups from receiving benefits (e.g., full or part-time college students were not eligible for benefits); reduced the amount of benefit received when calculating the benefit; or restricted or eliminated persons who were not "work-capable" (e.g., handicapped persons or pregnant women who could not work forty-five days consecutively were denied benefits).

Liberal Statutes are those that increase the amount of benefit calculated; protects certain groups from exclusion; or expands eligibility. There were no liberal statutes in this category.

Ideologically Ambiguous Statutes are those that were not clearly associated with liberal or conservative ideologies. For example, this group consisted of procedural issues, such as filing requirements, or administrative implementation of the law. This category also included laws that denied benefits for voluntary leave of employment. Since many of these laws or provisions involved other issues, the facts of the case would have been necessary to determine ideological direction; using facts of the case would make the classification endogenous and thus was not done.

Welfare Benefits constituted six categories: residency requirements, reimbursement, benefit restriction or limitation, benefit expansion, welfare fraud, and other.

Conservative Statutes are those that prohibit certain groups from receiving benefits (e.g., residency requirement) or limited the amount of benefits or amount of time benefits could be received.

Liberal Statutes are those that increase the amount of benefit calculated or expands eligibility. There were no liberal statutes in this category.

Ideologically Ambiguous Statutes are those that were not clearly associated with liberal or conservative ideologies. For example, this group consisted of welfare fraud; welfare reimbursement (e.g., estate to be given to state for repayment of welfare when recipient dies, lien on property); and other (e.g., amount hospitals should be reimbursed, tax on county government to pay for welfare).

Independent Variables (not described in text):

Divided Government Dichotomous variable equal to one for states in which the legislature and governor were controlled by different parties; zero otherwise.
    Source: *The Book of the States,* various years.

Method of Retention
Dichotomous variable equal to one for states where the legislature or governor *did not* retain justices, zero otherwise.

Source: *The Book of the States* Council of State Governments, Lexington, KY 1968–69; 1970–71; 1972–3; . . . 1994–95; *The American Bench*, Minneapolis: Reginald Bishop Foster and Associates 1977; 1978; 1979; 1985–86; 1987–88; 1989–90; . . . 1995–96.

Term Length
Dichotomous variable equal to one for states in which the length of term is above average (i.e., six years), zero otherwise.

Source: *The Book of the States*, various years.

Difficult Amendment Process
Dichotomous variable equal to one for states in which it requires two legislative sessions for a constitutional amendment to pass, zero otherwise.

Source: *The Book of the States*, various years.

Intermediate Appellate Court:
Dichotomous variable equal to one for states in the years for which there was an intermediate appellate court, zero otherwise.

Source: *The American Bench* and *Book of the States*, various years.

Constitutional Rights
Dichotomous variable equal to one for states with a constitutional right to vote provision, an equal protection provision, right to privacy provision or a freedom of speech provision, zero otherwise.

Source: The 50 State Constitutions. Computed by author

Independent State Grounds
Dichotomous variable equal to one when the court explicitly stated the opinion is based on independent state grounds, zero otherwise.

Source: Coded by author from court opinion.

Lower Court Ruling
Dichotomous variable equal to one when the lower court (i.e., trial or intermediate appellate court) declares the statute in question unconstitutional, zero otherwise.

Source: Coded by author from court opinion.

Standard of Review
Dichotomous variable equal to one when the state supreme court invoked strict scrutiny for standard of review, zero otherwise.

Lower Court Does not Participate
Dichotomous variable equal to one if a lower court (i.e., trial or intermediate appellate court) did not rule on the constitutionality of the statute or if the case went directly to the state supreme court, zero otherwise.

Notes

CHAPTER ONE

1. Page 1 in James C. Foster and Susan M. Leeson (1998) Constitutional Law Cases in Context: Volume II Civil Rights and Civil Liberties, New Jersey: Prentice Hall.

2. Bush and his attorneys appealed the Florida Supreme Court decision to the United States Supreme Court. The United States Supreme Court remanded the case to the Florida Supreme Court, instructing the state court to clarify their decision. Specifically, the United States Supreme Court told the Florida Supreme Court to explain whether or not the Florida Supreme Court was interpreting or making law. In the end, the United States Supreme Court made the final decision, which led to George W. Bush becoming the next president of the United States.

3. Jonathan Casper (1976) provides strong empirical support for the hypothesis that the Court is an independent actor, capable and willing to challenge lawmaking majorities and defend the rights of minorities and individuals. Robert Dahl and Richard Funston's empirical findings have also received criticism from David Adamany (1973), Paul Allen Beck (1976), and Bradley C. Canon and S. Sidney Ulmer (1976).

4. For example, see *Seminole Tribe v Florida* 515 U. S. 1125 (1996); *Florida Prepaid Postsecondary Education Expense Board v College Savings Bank and United States* 119 S. Ct. 2219 (1999); *Kimel et al., v. Florida Board of Regents et al.,* No. 98–971 (January 11, 2000); *Reno v Bossier Parish School Board* 98–405(January 2000); *Nixon et al. v. Shrink Missouri Government PAC et al.,* 98–963 (2000).

5. This notion of judicial review is what Kermit L. Hall (1984) called the "departmental theory" of judicial review.

CHAPTER TWO

1. With a few exceptions (e.g., New York), state courts of last resort are called the "state's supreme court." Thus, in this project, state supreme courts refer to the court of last resort.

2. Cases can also be certified from another court or another branch of government. Such instances were extremely rare in the cases examined in this project.

3. In this way, stage one and stage two are similar because they can both produce formal decisions with opinion; however, in stage one the court is simply deciding whether to rule on the substantive merits of the case.

4. But see Ulmer (1986) who found that background characteristics worked well to predict judicial behavior in the early twentieth century, but not in the second half of the twentieth century.

5. While the use of cumulative scaling and partisan affiliation to infer judicial preferences has become common practice in judicial politics, there are some serious limitations with these measures (see, e.g., Brace, Langer, and Hall 2000). Perhaps most problematic with using past voting or cumulative scaling techniques is the endogeniety problem inherent in these techniques. These estimates of judicial ideology are not independent measures of their preferences. Inferences about judicial preferences from partisan affiliation also are problematic because a simple dichotomous variable cannot adequately capture the range of preferences typically represented on a single court.

6. With the exception of the influence of the Solicitor General, Jeffrey A. Segal and Harold J. Spaeth (1993) refute alternative external explanations of judicial behavior.

7. Melinda Gann Hall (1998) has found that judicial elections are no less competitive than elections for the United States House of Representatives.

8. Early on, scholars demonstrated that the dockets of state supreme courts are responsive to conditions in the state's environment such as personal income, competition, and so forth (see, e.g., Atkins and Glick 1974). These studies, however, primarily focus on the aggregate docket of courts (i.e., number of cases docketed). Moreover, these studies do not consider strategic accounts of the agenda-setting process that may be at play. A more comprehensive model of agenda-setting might attenuate the results of earlier studies.

9. Later John F. Krol and Saul Brenner (1990) reexamined the hypothesis that judges engage in forward-looking voting (i.e., strategic or prediction strategies) when "deciding to decide" a case. They find support for previous studies with respect to an error-correcting strategy, but they find less support for the prediction strategy. They conclude that judges do not appear to be behaving in a strategic manner on votes to grant *certiorari*.

10. A recent study by John C. Kilwein and Richard A. Brisbin (1997) examines the hierarchical relationship between the state supreme courts and the United States Supreme Court, testing whether state supreme court justices vote in response to the preferences of the superior court. David R. Songer, Jeffrey A. Segal, and Charles M. Cameron (1994) also test a hierarchical relationship among courts, demonstrating a principal-agent relationship between the federal appellate courts and the United States Supreme Court. These hierarchical relationships are beyond the scope of this book.

11. This contention is reduced, however, when it is not an issue of constitutional nature before the Supreme Court, because it is less difficult for the Supreme Court to overturn nonconstitutional decisions and fewer actors are involved.

12. Note, however, that Jeffrey A. Segal (1997) offered strong evidence that casts doubt on the separation-of-powers argument with respect to the United States Supreme Court. According to Segal, Supreme Court justices vote sincerely without deference to Congress or the president in matters of statutory interpretation.

CHAPTER THREE

1. While there is an abundance of literature developing and testing theories about the motivations of members of the legislative and the executive branches, a discussion of these motivations is beyond the scope of this project.

2. The constitutional provision that was declared unconstitutional pertained to state libel prosecution and was found to be repugnant to the United States Constitution in light of *New York Times v Sullivan* 376 U. S. 254 (1964).

3. Lawrence Baum (1994) notes that legislative and gubernatorial retaliatory attacks on courts date back to the early nineteenth century.

4. Tsebelis (1990) applies this argument in international relations, however, his ideas can be appropriately applied to a study of the relationship between state supreme courts and their external political environment.

5. For the remainder of this project, state government refers to the state legislature and governor unless otherwise noted.

6. To avoid the cumbersome use of legislature and governor, state government and governmental actors refer to the legislature and governor and are used interchangeably throughout the book.

7. Similar constraints are estimated for each state supreme court during the period 1970–1993 for the agenda-setting stage of the analysis. See appendix for a complete description.

8. The primary limitation of excluding a litigant from the selection model is that this study cannot speak to litigant strategies to raise constitutional challenges before courts more sympathetic to the litigant's complaint. From my perspective, this limitation far outweighs the empirical and theoretical limitations associated with ignoring the selection stage.

9. Ideally we would want to be able to test a ratio of the distance between the preferences of the judge and ideology of the statute and the distance between the preferences of state government and the ideology of the statute. This would permit a more direct test of whether a judge is influenced by sincere preferences or strategic considerations. Such a test, however, requires one to make interpersonal comparisons of each actor's utility. This violates a fundamental premise of rational choice game theoretic models.

10. Scholars only recently have begun to evaluate the factors that explain the choice of legal doctrine.

11. Some of the constitutional challenges in these cases required state supreme courts to take original action. In other cases the lower court heard the case, but did not rule on the constitutionality of the statute. A variable identifying these cases was included in the models; however, no directional expectation was made.

CHAPTER FOUR

1. Because *Per Curium* opinions reflect the decision of the court, these cases also were eventually excluded from the analysis.

2. It is important to note that the high number of campaign and election cases generated in the initial searches and the high rate of elimination of these cases is due in large part to the type of searches Lexis-Nexis permits. For example, with campaign and election laws, it was necessary to use several different search languages on Lexis-Nexis to prevent the exclusion of relevant cases. Westlaw, however, utilizes a key number system that identifies cases by area of law and thus eliminates many of the irrelevant cases in the first round. For example, the Lexis-Nexis searches produced over five thousand cases for workers' compensation; fifteen hundred cases for unemployment compensation; and close to three thousand for welfare cases, compared to the small numbers produced by Westlaw's key number system. Thus, for these three areas of law, the searches were conducted using Westlaw, which was not available until late March 1998 as a pay-for-service arrangement through Rice University. I compared cases produced from WestLaw search and Lexis-Nexis search to make sure I had as close to an inclusive list as possible.

3. The author thanks Professor Jeff Yates (Ph.D., and, J.D.), an assistant professor of public law at the University of Georgia, and Russell Post (M.A., and J.D.), who is a practicing attorney specializing in constitutional law.

4. The author wishes to thank Kellie Butler, a Ph.D. candidate at Rice University, for assisting in the inter-coder reliability tests. The decision to include the standard of review employed by the court and the primary constitutional violation was made after coding the first thirty-five cases. As a result, inter-coder reliability tests were conducted on these characteristics for the remaining 343 cases.

5. Some cases were given to judicial scholars for external validation. I am grateful to Professor Paul Brace at Rice University, Professor Melinda Gann Hall at Michigan State University, and Professor Jeff Yates at University of Georgia.

6. States for which there were two cases on the docket in the same year were treated as having one case on the docket in that year. From a theoretical perspective, the question in this stage of the analysis concerns the forces contributing to a state having a case on its docket. Thus, the number of cases on the docket is not a concern at this time.

7. For a good example of a modified selection model see Meernik and Ignagni (1997).

8. Many statistical packages estimate the two stages of the James J. Heckman selection model simultaneously.

CHAPTER FIVE

1. There are reasons to expect that the relationship between ideological distance and the likelihood of reviewing and invalidating statutes would be conditional on the political settings and institutional rules. Recent evidence suggests that ideological distance is modified when it is more difficult for state government to retaliate against the court (Langer 1997). Alternative hypotheses about the conditioning impact of institutional rules and design are left for future study.

2. The difference in these findings could simply be due to the variation across models. The frequency of lower court involvement in deciding the constitutionality issue on liberal statutes was much higher than in conservative statutes.

3. Examination of votes to overturn liberal statutes was not possible because there were too few liberal statutes in this area of law.

4. As in the workers' compensation cases, there were too few liberal statutes in this area of law.

CHAPTER SIX

1. Arguably, the office of president could constitute a higher office than the United States Supreme Court.

2. Of course research by Hall (e.g., 1992) and Brace and Hall (e.g., 1990) has demonstrated state supreme court justices behave strategically with respect to the public, but only in death penalty cases. In more recent work, I have found evidence of strategic behavior in response to chief justices, *amici* participants, and the general public in the area of workers' compensation (Langer 1999).

References

Abrahamson, Shirley S. 1996. "Remarks of the Hon. Shirley S. Abrahamson before the American Bar Association Commission on Separation of Powers and Judicial Independence." *St. John's Journal of Legal Commentary* 12:69–88.

Abrahamson, Shirley S., and Robert L. Hughes. 1991. "The William B. Lockhart Lecture: Shall We Dance? Steps for Legislators and Judges in Statutory Interpretation." *Minnesota Law Review* 75:1045–094.

Achen, Christopher H. 1986. *The Statistical Analysis of Quasi-Experiments.* Berkeley: University of California Press.

Adamany, David. 1973. "Law and Society: Legitimacy, Realigning Elections, and the Supreme Court." *Wisconsin Law Review* 3:790–846.

Aldrich, John H., and Forrest D. Nelson. 1984. *Linear Probability, Logit, and Probit Models.* Beverly Hills: Sage Publications.

Allison, Paul D. 1984. *Event History Analysis: Regression for Longitudinal Event Data.* Beverly Hills: Sage Publications.

Arnold, Douglas R. 1990. *The Logic of Congressional Action,* New Haven: Yale University Press.

Atkins, Burton M., and Henry R. Glick. 1976. "Environmental and Structural Variables as Determinants of Issues in State Courts of Last Resort." *American Journal of Political Science* 20:97–115.

Baird, Douglas G., Robert H. Gertner, and Randal C. Picker. 1994. *Game Theory and the Law.* Cambridge, MA: Harvard University Press.

Bator, Paul M. 1990. "The Constitution as Architecture: Legislative and Administrative Courts Under Article III." *Indiana Law Journal* 65:233–271.

Baum, Lawrence. 1977. "Policy Goals in Judicial Gate-Keeping: A Proximity Model of Discretionary Jurisdiction." *American Journal of Political Science* 21:13–36.

———. 1997. *The Puzzle of Judicial Behavior.* Ann Arbor: University of Michigan Press.

———. 1994. *American Courts.* 3 ed. Boston: Houghton Mifflin Company.

———. 1985. *The Supreme Court, 2nd ed.* Washington, D.C.: CQ Press.

————. 1979. "Judicial Demand-Screening and Decisions on the Merits." *American Politics Quarterly* 7:109–119.

Baumgartner, Frank R., and Bryan D. Jones. 1993. *Agendas and Instability in American Politics*. Chicago: University of Chicago Press.

Beck, Paul Allen. 1976. "Critical Elections and the Supreme Court: Putting the Cart After the Horse." *American Political Science Review* 70:930–932.

Beck, Nathaniel and Jonathan Katz. 1995. "What to Do (and Not to Do) with Time-Series Cross Section Data in Comparative Politics." *American Political Science Review* 89: 34–47.

Berry, William D., Evan J. Ringquist, Richard C. Fording, and Russell L. Hanson. 1998. "Measuring Citizen and Government Ideology in the American States, 1960–93." *American Journal of Political Science* 42:327–348.

Berry, William D., and Francis Stokes Berry. 1990. "State Lottery Adoptions as Policy Innovations: An Event History Analysis." *American Political Science Review* 84:395–415.

Bickel, Alexander. 1962. *The Least Dangerous Branch*. New York: Bobbs-Merril.

Blue, Daniel. 1991. "Legislators and Judges: Minding the Riff. *State Legislatures* 17:34–35.

Bond, Jon R., and Richard Fleisher. 1990. *The President in the Legislative Arena*. Chicago: The University of Chicago Press.

Boucher, Robert and Jeffrey A. Segal. 1995. "Supreme Court Justices as Strategic Decision Makers: Offensive Grants and Defensive Denials on the Vincent Court." *Journal of Politics* 57:54–70.

Brace, Paul and Barbara Hinckley. 1992. *Follow the Leader: Opinion Polls and the Modern Presidents*. New York: Basic Books.

Brace, Paul, and Melinda Gann Hall. 1997. "The Interplay of Preferences, Case Facts, Context, and Rules in the Politics of Judicial Choice." *Journal of Politics* 59:1206–1231.

————. 1995. "Studying Courts Comparatively: The View from The American States." *Political Research Quarterly* 48:5–29.

————. 1993. "Integrated Models of Judicial Dissent." *Journal of Politics* 55:914–35.

————. 1990. "Neo-Institutionalism and Dissent in State Supreme Courts." *Journal of Politics* 52:54–70.

Brace, Paul and Jewett Aubrey. 1995. "The State of State Politics Research." *Political Research Quarterly* 48:643–811.

Brace, Paul, Melinda Gann Hall, and Laura Langer. 2001. "Placing Courts in State Politics." *State Politics and Policy Quarterly*. 1:81–108.

————. 1999. "Judicial Choice and the Politics of Abortion: Institutions, Context, and the Autonomy of Courts." *Albany Law Review* (1999) 62:1265–1302.

Brace, Paul, Laura Langer, and Melinda Gann Hall. 2000. "Measuring the Preferences of State Supreme Court Judges." *Journal of Politics* 62:387–413.

Brace, Paul and Laura Langer. (2001). "The Other Face of Judicial Power: State Supreme Courts and Abortion in the American States. Paper presented at the Midwest Political Science Association Annual Mtg. Chicago, IL April, 2001.

Breen, Richard. 1996. *Regression Models: Censored, Sample Selected, or Truncated Data.* London: Sage Publications, Inc.

Brenner, Saul. 1980. "Fluidity on the United States Supreme Court: A Reexamination." *American Journal of Political Science* 24:526–535.

————. 1979. "The New Certiorari Game." *Journal of Politics* 41:649–55.

Brenner, Saul, and John F. Krol. 1989. "Strategies in Certiorari Voting on the United States Supreme Court." *Journal of Politics* 51:828–40.

Brenner, Saul, and Harold J. Spaeth. 1995. *Stare Indecisis: The Alteration of Precedent on the Supreme Court, 1946–1992.* New York: Cambridge University Press.

Cain, Bruce, John Ferejohn, and Morris Fiorina. 1987. *The Personal Vote: Constituency Service and Electoral Independence.* Cambridge, MA: Harvard University Press.

Caldeira, Gregory A. 1983. "On the Reputation of State Supreme Courts." *Political Behavior* 5:83–108.

Caldeira, Gregory A., and John R. Wright. 1998. "Lobbying for Justice: Organized Interests, Supreme Court Nominations, and the United States Senate." *American Journal of Political Science* 42:499–523.

————. 1988. "Organized Interests and Agenda Setting in the U.S. Supreme Court." *American Political Science Review* 82:1109–1127.

Cameron, Charles M., Albert D. Cover, and Jeffrey A. Segal. 1990. "Senate Voting on Supreme Court Nominees: A Neoinstitutional Model." *American Political Science Review* 84:525–534.

Canon, Bradley C. 1983. "Defining the Dimensions of Judicial Activism." *Judicature* 66:236–247.

Canon, Bradley C., and S. Sidney Ulmer. 1976. "The Supreme Court and Critical Elections: A Dissent." *American Political Science Review* 70:1215–1218.

Casper, Jonathan. 1976. "The Supreme Court and National Policy Making." *American Political Science Review* 70:50–63.

Champagne, Anthony and Judith Haydel. 1993. *Judicial Reform in the States.* Lanham, MD: University Press of America.

Clinton, Robert Lowry. 1989. *Marbury v. Madison and Judicial Review*. Kansas: University Press of Kansas.

Cohen, Jeffrey E. 1997. *Presidential Responsiveness and Public Policy-Making*. Ann Arbor: The University of Michigan Press.

Cook, Beverly B. 1973. "Sentencing Behavior of Federal Judges: Draft Cases—1972." *University of Cincinnati Law Review* 42:597–633.

Dahl, Robert. 1989. "The Supreme Court's Role in National Policy-Making." In *American Court Systems*. Edited by Sheldon Goldman and Austin Sarat. *2 ed*. Reprint, New York: Longman.

———. 1957. "Decisionmaking in a Democracy: The Supreme Court as a National Policymaker." *Journal of Public Law* 6:279–295.

Danelski, David. 1966. "Values as Variables in Judicial Decision-Making: Notes Toward a Theory." *Vanderbilt Law Review* 19:721–740.

Downs, Anthony. 1957. *An Economic Theory of Democracy*, New York: HarperCollins Publishers, Inc.

Dubois, L. Philip. 1980. *From Ballot to Bench: Judicial Elections and The Quest for Accountability*. Austin, Texas: University of Texas Press.

Ducat, Craig R. 1978. *Modes of Constitutional Interpretation*. St. Paul: West Publishing Company.

Ducat, Craig R., and Robert L. Dudley. 1987. "Dimensions Underlying Economic Policymaking in the Early and Later Burger Courts." *Journal of Politics* 49:521–539.

Dye, Thomas R., and L. Harmon Zeigler. 1972. *The Irony of Democracy: An Uncommon Introduction to American Politics*. 2d ed. Belmont, California: Duxbury Press.

Emmert, Craig F. 1992. "An Integrated Case-Related Model of Judicial Decisionmaking: Explaining State Supreme Court Decisions in Judicial Review Cases." *Journal of Politics* 54:543–552.

Emmert, Craig F., and Carol Ann Traut. 1994. "The California Supreme Court and the Death Penalty. *American Politics Quarterly* 22:41–61.

Epstein, Lee and Carol Mershon. 1996. "Measuring Political Preferences." *American Journal of Political Science* 40:261–294.

Epstein, Lee and Jack Knight. 1998. *The Choices Justices Make*. Washington, D.C.: CQ Press.

Epstein, Lee, and Thomas G. Walker. 1995. "The Role of The Supreme Court in American Society: Playing the Reconstruction Game." In *Contemplating Courts*. Edited by Lee Epstein. Washington D.C.: CQ Press.

Erikson, Robert S., Gerald C. Wright, and John P. McIver. 1993. *Statehouse Democracy*. Cambridge, England: Cambridge University.

Eskridge, William N. Jr. 1991. "Overriding Supreme Court Statutory Interpretation Decisions." *Yale Law Journal* 101:825–41.

Fair, Daryl R. 1967. "An Experimental Application of Scalogram Analysis to State Supreme Court Decisions." *Wisconsin Law Review* 1967:449–459.

Federalist No. 51 "The Structure of the Government Must Furnish the Proper Checks and Balances Between the Different Departments." from the New York Packet. Friday, Feb. 8, 1788 *Hamilton or Madison* Publius.

Federalist No. 78 "The Judiciary Department." From McLean's Edition, New York. 1788 *Hamilton* Publius.

Feeley, Malcolm, M. 1971. "Research Note: Another Look at the 'Party Variable' in Judicial Decision-Making." *Polity* 4:91–104.

Fenno, Richard F. 1978. *Home Style House Members in Their Districts*. Boston, MA: Little, Brown, and Company.

———. 1973. *Congressmen in Committees*. Boston, MA: Little, Brown, and Company.

Ferejohn, John and Charles F. Shipan. 1990. "Congressional Influence on Bureaucracy." *Journal of Law, Economics, and Organization* 6(Special Issue): 1–27.

Fino, Susan. 1987. "Judicial Federalism and Equality Guarantees in State Supreme Courts." *Publius* 17:51–67.

Flemming, Roy B., and B. Dan Wood. 1997. "The Public and the Supreme Court: Individual Justice Responsiveness to American Policy Moods." *American Journal of Political Science* 41:468–498.

Foster, James C. and Susan M. Leeson. 1998. "Constitutional Law Cases in Context: Volume II Civil Rights and Civil Liberties." Upper Saddle River, New Jersey: Prentice Hall.

Frank, Jerome. 1950. *Courts on Trial: Myth and Reality in American Jurisprudence*. Princeton: Princeton University Press.

Friedelbaum, Stanley H. 1982. "Supreme Courts in State Judicial Administration." In *State Supreme Courts: Policymakers In The Federal System*. Edited by Mary Cornelia Porter and G. Alan Tarr. Westport, CT: Greenwood Press.

Funston, Richard. 1975. "The Supreme Court and Critical Elections." *American Political Science Review* 69:795–811.

Galanter, Marc. 1974. "Why the 'Haves' Come Out Ahead: Speculations on the Limits of Legal Change." *Law and Society Review* 31:4–71.

Gates, John. 1987. "Partisan realignment, unconstitutional state policies, and the U.S. Supreme Court." *American Journal of Political Science* 31:259–280.

Gely, Rafael, and Pablo T. Spiller. 1992. "The Political Economy of Supreme Court Constitutional Decisions: The Case of Roosevelt's Court-Packing Plan." *International Review of Law and Economics* 12:45–67.

———. 1990. "A Rational Choice Theory of Supreme Court Decision Making With Application to the *State Farm* and *Grove City* Cases." *Journal of Law, Economics, and Organizations* 6:263–300.

Gerber, Elizabeth. 1996. "Legislatures, Initiatives, and Representation: The Effects of Legislative Institutions on Policy." *Political Research Quarterly* 49:263–286.

Gibson, James L. 1978. "Judges' Role Orientations, Attitudes, and Decisions: An Interactive Model." *American Political Science Review* 72:911–924.

Giles, Micheal W., and Thomas G. Walker. 1975. "Judicial Policy-Making and Southern Social Segregation." *Journal of Politics* 37:917–936.

Glick, Henry R. 1992. *The Right to Die: Policy Innovation and its Consequences.* New York: Columbia Press.

———. 1991. "Policy Making and State Supreme Courts." In *The American Courts.* Edited by John B. Gates and Charles A. Johnson. Washington, D.C.: CQ Press.

Glick, Henry R., and Craig F. Emmert. 1987. "Selection Systems and Judicial Characteristics: the Recruitment of State Supreme Court Judges." *Judicature* 70:228–235.

Glick, Henry R., and George W. Pruet, Jr. 1986. "Dissent in State Supreme Courts: Patterns and Correlates of Conflict." In *Judicial Conflict and Consensus: Behavioral Studies of American Appellate Courts.* Edited by Sheldon Goldman and Charles Lamb. Lexington, KY: University Press of Kentucky.

Glick, Henry R., and Kenneth N. Vines. 1973. *State Court Systems.* Englewood Cliffs, New Jersey: Prentice Hall.

Goldman, Sheldon. 1997. *Picking Federal Judges: Lower Court Selection From Roosevelt Through Reagan* New Haven: Yale University Press.

Goldstein, Leslie Friedman. 1995. "By Consent of the Governed: Directions in Constitutional Theory." In *Contemplating Courts.* Edited by Lee Epstein. Washington D.C.: CQ Press.

Graham, Barbara Luck. 1990. "Do Judicial Selection Systems Matter?" *American Politics Quarterly* 18:316–336.

Green, William H. 1993. *Econometric Analysis.* 2d ed. Englewood Cliffs, NJ: Prentice Hall.

Hagle, Timothy M., and Glenn E. Mitchell II. 1992. "Goodness of Fit Measures for Probit and Logit." *American Journal of Political Science* 36:162–4.

Hagle, Timothy M., and Harold J. Spaeth. 1992. "The Emergence of a New Ideology: The Business Decisions of the Burger Court." *Journal of Politics* 54:120–134.

Hahn, Harlan and Sheldon Kamieniecki. 1987. *Referendum Voting: Social Status and Policy Preferences.* New York: Greenwood Press.

Haines, Charles G. 1922. "General Observations on the Effects of Personal, Political, and Economic Interests in the Decisions of Judges." *Illinois Law Review* 17:96–116.

Hall, Kermit L. 1984. *The Supreme Court and Judicial Review in American History.* Washington, D.C.: American Historical Society.

Hall, Melinda Gann. 1999. "State Judicial Politics: Rules, Structures, and the Political Game." In *American State and Local Politics.* Edited by Ronald E. Weber and Paul Brace, 114–138. New York: Chatham House Publishers.

———. 1998. "Competition in Judicial Elections, 1980–1985." Paper presented at the American Political Science Association, Boston Massachusetts.

———. 1995. "Justices as Representatives: Elections and Judicial Politics in the American States." *American Politics Quarterly* 23:485–503.

———. 1992. "Electoral Politics and Strategic Voting in State Supreme Courts." *Journal of Politics* 54:427–46.

———. 1987. "Constituent Influence in State Supreme Courts: Conceptual Notes and a Case Study." *Journal of Politics* 49:1114–1121.

Hall, Melinda Gann, and Paul Brace. 1994. "The Vicissitudes of Death by Decree: Forces Influencing Capital Punishment Decision Making in State Supreme Courts." *Social Science Quarterly* 75:136–51.

———. 1992. "Toward an Integrated Model of Judicial Voting Behavior." *American Politics Quarterly* 20:147–168.

———. 1989. "Order in the Courts: A Neo-Institutional Approach to Judicial Consensus." *Western Political Quarterly* 42:391–407.

Hammons, Christopher. 1999. "Was James Madison Wrong? Rethinking the American Preference for Short, Framework-Oriented Constitutions." *American Political Science Review* 93:837–849.

Harrington, Christine B., and Daniel S. Ward. 1995. "Patterns of Appellate Litigants." In *Contemplating Courts.* Edited by Lee Epstein, 206–226. Washington D.C.: CQ Press.

Harrison, Russell S. and G. Alan Tarr. 1996. "School Finance and Inequality in New Jersey." In Constitutional Politics in the States: Contemporary Controversies and Historical Patterns. Edited by G. Alan Tarr. Westport, CT: Greenwood Press.

Heckman, James J. 1979. "Sample Selection Bias as a Specification Error." *Econometrica* 47 (January):153–162.

Hinich, Melvin and Michael Munger. 1997. *Analytical Politics*. New York: Cambridge University Press.

Horowitz, Donald L. 1977. *The Courts and Social Policy*. Washington, D.C.: Brookings Institution.

Howard, J. Woodford. 1968. "On the Fluidity of Judicial Choice." *American Political Science Review* 62:43–57.

Hunzeker, Donna. 1990. "Legislative-Judicial Relations: Seeking a New Partnership." *State Legislative Reports* Denver, CO: National Conference of State Legislatures. Vol. 15, No. 14 July.

James, Bernard. 1999. "The States' Rights Cases Provoke Fire." *National Law Journal* (August 16, 1999): 10–18.

Kaufman, Robert L. 1996. "Comparing Effects in Dichotomous Logistic Regression: A Variety of Standardized Coefficients." *Social Science Quarterly* 77:90–109.

Kaye, Judith S. 1995. "Brennan Lecture: State Courts at the Dawn of a New Century: Common Law Courts Reading Statutes and Constitutions." New York University Law Review. 70:1–36.

Key, V. O. 1961. *Public Opinion and American Democracy*. New York: Knopf.

Kilwein, John C. and Richard A. Brisbin Jr. 1997. "Policy Convergence in a Federal Judicial System: The Application of Intensified Scrutiny Doctrines by State Supreme Courts." *American Journal of Political Science* 41:122–148.

Kingdon, John W. 1981. *Congressmen's Voting Decisions*. 2d ed. New York: Harper and Row.

Krol, John F., and Saul Brenner. 1990. "Strategies in Certiorari Voting on the United States Supreme Court." *Western Political Quarterly*, 335–342.

Langer, Laura. 1999. "Does the Chief Justice on State Courts of Last Resort Shape Judicial Review? The Case of Workers' Compensation." Paper presented at the American Political Science Association Annual Meeting, Atlanta, Georgia. Paper won the American Judicature Award, 2000.

———. 1998. "State Supreme Courts and Countermajoritarian Behavior." Ph.D diss., Florida State University.

———. 1997. "State Supreme Courts and Countermajoritarian Behavior: Strategic or Sincere?" Paper presented at the Conference of the Scientific Study of Judicial Politics, Emory University, Atlanta, Georgia, November.

Lascher, Edward L. Jr., Michael G. Hagen, and Steven A. Rochlin. 1996. "Gun Behind the Door? Ballot Initiatives, State Policies and Public Opinion." *Journal of Politics* 58:760–775.

Liao, Tim Futing. 1994. *Interpreting Probability Models: Logit, Probit, and Other Generalized Linear Models.* Sage University Paper #101 Thousand Oaks, CA: Sage.

Lindblom, Charles E. 1968. *The Policy-Making Process.* Englewood Cliffs, NJ: Prentice-Hall, Inc.

Lowi, Theodore, J. 1964. "American Business, Public Policy, Case-Studies, and Political Theory." *World Politics* 16:

Lutz, Donald L. 1994. "Toward a Theory of Constitutional Amendment." *American Political Science Review* 88:355–370.

Maddala, G. S. 1983. *Limited-Dependent and Qualitative Variables in Econometrics.* Cambridge: Cambridge University Press.

Maltzman, Forrest and Paul J. Wahlbeck. 1996. "Inside the U.S. Supreme Court: The Reliability of the Justices' Conference Records." *Journal of Politics* 58:528–539.

Marks Brian. 1989. *"A Model of Judicial Influence on Congressional Policymaking: Grove City College v. Bell."* Ph.D. diss., Washington University.

Marshall, Thomas. 1989. *Public Opinion and the Supreme Court.* New York: Longman.

Mayhew, David R. 1974. *Congress: The Electoral Connection.* New Haven: Yale University Press.

Meernik, James and Joseph Ignagni. 1997. "Judicial Review and Coordinate Construction of the Constitution." *American Journal of Political Science.* 41:447–467.

Mezey, Michael L. 1993. "Legislatures: Individual Purpose and Institutional Performance." In Ada W. Finifter. Editor *Political Science: The State of the Discipline.* Washington, DC: American Political Science Association.

Mishler, William, and Reginald S. Sheehan. 1996. "Public Opinion, the Attitudinal Model, and Supreme Court Decision Making: A Micro-Analytic Perspective." *Journal of Politics* 58:169–200.

———. 1993. "The Supreme Court as a Countermajoritarian Institution?" *American Political Science Review* 87:87–101.

Moe, Terry M. 1993. "Presidents, Institutions, and Theory." In *Researching the Presidency: Vital Questions, New Approaches.* Editors George C. Edwards III, John H. Kessel, and Bert A. Rockman.

Murphy, Walter. 1964. *Elements of Judicial Strategy.* Chicago: University of Chicago Press.

Mutch, Robert E. 1988. *Campaigns, Congress, and Courts: The Making of Federal Campaign Finance Law.* New York: Praeger.

Norpoth, Helmut, Jeffrey Segal, William Mishler, and Reginald S. Sheehan. 1994. "Popular Influence on Supreme Court Decisions." *American Political Science Review* 88:711–24.

North, Douglass C. 1990. *Institutions, Institutional Change, and Economic Performance* New York: Cambridge Cambridge University Press

Olson, Mancur. 1965. *The Logic of Collective Action; Public Goods and the Theory of Groups.* Cambridge, MA: Harvard University Press

Page, Benjamin I., and Robert Y. Shapiro. 1983. "Effects of Public Opinion on Policy." *American Political Science Review* 77:175–90.

Palmer, Jan. 1982. "An Economic analysis of the U.S. Supreme Court's *certiorari* decisions." *Public Choice* 39:387–398.

Perry, H. W. 1991. *Deciding to Decide: Agenda Setting in the United States Supreme Court.* Cambridge, MA: Harvard University Press.

Peters, Ellen Ash. "Remarks at the State of the Judiciary." State of Connecticut. March 8, 1995.

Plott, Charles. 1991a. "Will Economics become an Experimental Science?" *Southern Economic Journal* 57:901–20.

Polsby, Nelson. 1984. *Political Innovation.* New Haven: Yale University Press.

Pritchett, C. Herman. 1948. *The Roosevelt Court: A Study of Judicial Votes and Values.* New York: Macmillan.

———. 1941. "Division of Opinion Among Justices on the U.S. Supreme Court, 1939–1941." *American Political Science Review* 25:890–898.

Provine, Doris Marie. 1980. *Case Selection in the United States Supreme Court.* Chicago: University of Chicago Press.

Ragsdale, Lyn. 1996. *Vital Statistics on The Presidency: Washington to Clinton.* Washington D.C.: Congressional Quarterly Inc.

Rathjen, Gregory J., and Harold J. Spaeth. 1990. "Denial of Access and Ideological Preferences: An Analysis of the Voting Behavior of the Burger Court Justices 1969–1976." In *Studies in United States Supreme Court Behavior.* Edited by Harold Spaeth and Saul Brenner, 24–43. New York: Garland Publisher.

———. 1979 "Access to the Federal Courts: An Analysis of Burger Court Policy Making." *American Journal of Political Science* 23:361–364.

Ripley, Randall B. 1983. *Congress: Process and Policy.* 3d ed. New York: W. W. Norton and Company.

Rivers, Douglas, and Nancy Rose. 1985. "Passing the President's Program: Public Opinion and Presidential Influence in Congress." *American Journal of Political Science* 29:183–96.

Rohde, David W. 1972. "Policy Goals, Strategic Choice and Majority Opinion Assignments in the U.S. Supreme Court." *American Journal of Political Science* 16:652–657.

Rohde, David W., and Harold J. Spaeth. 1976. *Supreme Court Decision Making.* San Francisco: W. H. Freeman and Company.

Rogers, James R. 2001. "Information and Judicial Review: A Signaling Game of Legislative-Judicial Interaction." *American Journal of Politics* 45:84–99.

Rowland, C. K., Donald Songer, and Robert A. Carp. 1988. "Presidential Effects on Criminal Justice Policy in the Lower Federal Courts: The Reagan Judges." *Law and Society Review* 22:191–200.

Schattschneider, E. E. 1960. *The Semisovereign People.* New York: Harcourt Brace Jovanovich College Publishers.

Schlesinger, Joseph A. 1991. *Political Parties and The Winning of Office.* Ann Arbor: University of Michigan Press.

———. 1966. *Ambition and Politics.* Chicago: Rand McNally.

Schubert, Glendon A. 1965. *The Judicial Mind: The Attitudes and Ideologies of Supreme Court Justices, 1946–1963.* Evanston, IL: Northwestern University Press.

———. 1964. *Judicial Behavior: A Reader in Theory and Research.* Chicago: Rand McNally.

———. 1962. "The 1960 Term of the Supreme Court: A Psychological Analysis." *American Political Science Review* 56:90–107.

———. 1959. *Quantitative Analysis of Judicial Behavior.* Glencoe, IL: The Free Press.

Schumpeter, Joseph A. 1942. *Capitalism, Socialism, and Democracy.* New York: Harper and Brothers.

Segal, Jeffrey A. 1997. "Separation-of-Powers Games in the Positive Theory of Congress and Courts." *American Political Science Review* 91: 28–44.

Segal, Jeffrey A., and Albert D. Cover. 1989. "Ideological Values and the Votes of U.S. Supreme Court Justices." *American Political Science Review* 83:557–65.

Segal, Jeffrey A., and Harold J. Spaeth. 1996. "The Influence of *Stare Decisis* on the Votes of United States Supreme Court Justices." *American Journal of Political Science* 40:971–1003.

———. 1993. *The Supreme Court and the Attitudinal Model.* New York: Cambridge University Press.

Segal, Jeffrey A., Charles M. Cameron, and Albert D. Cover. 1992. "A Spatial Model of Roll Call Voting: Senators, Constituents, Presidents and Interest Groups in Supreme Court Confirmations." *American Journal of Political Science* 36:96–121.

Segal, Jeffrey A., Lee Epstein, Charles M. Cameron, and Harold J. Spaeth. 1995. "Ideological Values and the Votes of U.S. Supreme Court Justices Revisted." *Journal of Politics* 57:812–823.

———. 1987. "Judicial Review and the Supreme Court of Washington, 1890–1986." *Publius: The Journal of Federalism* 17:69–89.

Sheldon, Charles H., and Linda S. Maule. 1997. *Choosing Justice: The Recruitment of State and Federal Judges.* Pullman, Washington: Washington State University Press.

Shepsle, Kenneth A., and Mark S. Bonchek. 1997. *Analyzing Politics: Rationality, Behavior, and Institutions.* New York: W. W. Norton & Company.

Shipman, Charles R. 1997. *Designing Judicial Review: Interest Groups, Congress, and Communications Policy.* Ann Arbor: University of Michigan Press.

Sinclair, Barbara. 1993. "Studying Presidential Leadership." *Researching the Presidency: Vital Questions, News Approaches.* Editors George C. Edwards III, John H. Kessel, and Bert A. Rockman.

Songer, Donald R., and Sue Davis. 1990. "The Impact of Party and Region on Voting Decision in the United States Courts of Appeals, 1955–1986." *Western Political Quarterly* 43:317–334.

Songer, Donald R., and Ashlyn Kuersten. 1995. "The Success of Amici in State Supreme Courts." *Political Research Quarterly* 48:31–42.

Songer, David R., Jeffrey A. Segal, and Charles M. Cameron. 1994. "The Hierarchy of Justice: Testing a Principal-Agent Perspective on Supreme Court-Circuit Court Interactions." *American Journal of Political Science* 38:673–95.

Spaeth, Harold J. 1979. *Supreme Court Policy Making: Explanation and Prediction.* San Francisco: W. H. Freeman and Company.

———. 1963a. "An Analysis of Judicial Attitudes in the Labor Relations Decisions of the Warren Court." *Midwest Journal of Political Science* 5:165–180.

———. 1963b. "Warren Court Attitudes Toward Business: The "B" Scale." In *Judicial Decision Making.* Edited by Glendon Schubert, 79–108. New York: Free Press.

Spaeth, Harold J., and Jeffrey A. Segal. 1999. *Majority Rule or Minority Will: Adherence to Precedent on the U.S. Supreme Court.* New York: Cambridge University Press.

Spiller, Pablo T., and Rafael Gely. 1992. "Congressional Control or Judicial Independence: The Determinants of U.S. Supreme Court Labor-Relations Decisions, 1949–1988." *RAND Journal of Economics* 23:463–492.

Spiller, Pablo T., and Matthew L. Spitzer. 1992. "Judicial Choice of Legal Doctrines." *Journal of Law, Economics and Organizations* 8:8–46.

Stimson, James A. 1985. "Regression in Space and Time: A Statistical Essay." *American Journal of Political Science* 29:914–47.

Stumpf, Harry P. 1998. *American Judicial Politics.* San Diego: Harcourt Brace Jovanovich.

Stumpf, Harry P., and John H. Culver. 1992. *The Politics of State Courts* New York: Longman Publishing Group.

Tanenhaus, Joseph, Marvin Schick, Matthew Muraskin, and Daniel Rosen. 1963. "The Supreme Court's Certiorari Jurisdiction: Cue Theory." In *Judicial Decision-Making.* Edited by Glendon Schubert. New York: Macmillan.

Tarr, G. Alan. 1998. *Understanding State Constitutions.* Princeton: Princeton University Press.

———. 1996. *Constitutional Politics in the States: Contemporary Controversies and Historical Patterns.* Westport: Greenwood Press.

Tarr, Alan G., and Mary Cornelia Aldis Porter. 1988. *State Supreme Courts in State and Nation.* New Haven: Yale University Press.

———. 1982. (eds.) *State Supreme Courts: Policymakers In The Federal System.* Westport, Connecticut: Greenwood Press.

Tate, C. Neal. 1981. "Personal Attribute Models of Voting Behavior of United States Supreme Court Justices: Liberalism in Civil Liberties and Economic Decisions, 1946–1978. *American Political Science Review* 75:355–67.

Tate, C. Neal and Roger Handberg. 1991. "Time Binding and Theory Building in Personal Attribute Model of Supreme Court Voting Behavior, 1916–88." *American Journal of Political Science* 35:460–480.

Teger, Stuart H., and Douglas Kosinski. 1980. "The Cue Theory of Supreme Court Certiorari Jurisdiction: A Reconsideration." *Journal of Politics* 42:834–846.

Tsebelis, George. 900. *Nested Games: Rational Choice in Comparative Politics.* Berkeley: University of California Press.

The American Bench: Judges of the Nation. Various Years. Sacramento: Reginald Bishop Forster.

The Book of the States. Various Years. Lexington, KY: Council of State Government.

Ulmer, S. Sidney. 1984. "The Supreme Court's Certiorari Decisions: Conflict as a Predictive Variable." *American Political Science Review* 78:901–911.

———. 1983. "Conflict with Supreme Court Precedent and the Granting of Plenary Review." *Journal of Politics* 45:474–478.

———. 1978. "Selecting Cases for Supreme Court Review: An Underdog Model." *American Political Science Review* 72:902–910.

———. 1973. "Social Background as an Indicator to the Votes of Supreme Court Justices in Criminal Cases." *Midwest Journal of Political Science* 17:622–30.

————. 1972. "The Decision to Grant Certiorari as an Indicator to Decision 'On the Merits.'" *Polity* 4:429–447.

————. 1962. "The Political Party Variable in the Michigan Supreme Court." *Journal of Public Law* 11:352–62.

————. 1960. "Supreme Court Behavior and Civil Rights." *Western Political Quarterly* 13:288–

Vines, Kenneth N. 1964. "Federal District Judges and Race Relations Cases in the South." *Journal of Politics* 26:337–357.

Walker, Jack L. 1977. "Setting the Agenda in the U.S. Senate." *British Journal of Political Science* 7:423–445.

Watson, Richard A., and Rondal G. Downing. 1969. *The Politics of the Bench and Bar.* New York: Wiley.

Wildavsky, Aaron. 1966. "The Two Presidencies." *Trans-Action* 4:7–14.

Wise, Dan. 1999. "N.H. Forum Debates Judicial Independence." New Hampshire Bar News. Vol. 10 (June 2, 1999): 1, 22–25.

Weingast Barry . 1996. A New handbook of Political Science. Oxford University Press, and Political Institutions; Rational Choice Perspectives. Pages 167–190. Ed.(Robert Goodin, Hans-Dieter Klingemann).

Index

Abrahamson, Shirley, 11, 15
Accountability: judicial, 3; to public, 3; theories on, xiii
Achen, Christopher, 86, 87
Agenda-setting stage of review, xiv, xv, 16, 20–22, 21*fig*, 24, 25, 27–28, 139*n3*; campaign and election law and, 89–94; constitutional challenges and, 20, 22; control of docket in, 20; decisions on taking cases, 20; dependent variables for, 85–86; divided government and, 48, 90*tab*, 91*tab*; docketed judicial review cases and, 47, 48, 90*tab*; expectations of, 47–50; as gatekeeping power, 20; ideological distance and, 90*tab*, 91*tab*; judicial behavior and, 19; policy options and, 47; power in, 3; preferences of state government and, 47–48; results for, 89–94; retention issues and, 49, 90*tab*, 91*tab*, 93; rights guaranteed by state constitutions and, 49–50; role of preferences in, 25; state constitution amendment, 90*tab*, 91*tab*; term length and, 49, 90*tab*, 91*tab*; unemployment compensation law and, 108–111; welfare law and, 115–118; worker's compensation law and, 101–104, 103*tab*
Alabama: amendment procedure in, 67*tab*; campaign and election law in, 75*tab*; intermediate appellate court in, 67*tab*; judicial retention in, 65*tab*; state supreme court in, 44, 68*tab*; worker's compensation law cases, 78*tab*, 79*tab*, 80*tab*, 81*tab*, 82*tab*
Alaska: amendment procedure in, 67*tab*; campaign and election law in, 75*tab*; intermediate appellate court in, 67*tab*; judicial retention in, 65*tab*; state supreme court in, 68*tab*; unemployment compensation law cases, 83*tab*; worker's compensation law cases, 78*tab*, 79*tab*, 80*tab*, 81*tab*, 82*tab*
Aldrich, John, 86
Allison, Paul, 85
Arizona: intermediate appellate court in, 67*tab*; judicial retention in, 65*tab*; state supreme court in, 68*tab*; worker's compensation law cases, 77*tab*, 78*tab*, 79*tab*, 81*tab*
Arkansas: campaign and election law in, 75*tab*; intermediate appellate court in, 67*tab*; judicial retention in, 65*tab*; state supreme court in, 68*tab*; worker's compensation law cases, 78*tab*, 80*tab*
Arnold, Douglas, 34, 55
Atkins, Burton, 94

Baird, Douglas, 129
Bator, Paul, 5
Baum, Lawrence, 9, 15, 22, 24, 25, 27, 49, 134, 141*n3*
Baumgartner, Frank, 53
Berry, William, 85
Blue, Daniel, 11, 35
Bonchek, Mark, 28, 34

159